Behavioural Finance

Wiley Finance Series

Behavioural Finance

Insights into Irrational Minds and Markets

James Montier

JOHN WILEY & SONS, LTD

Other Wiley Editorial Offices
John Wiley & Sons Inc., 111 River Street,
Hoboken, NJ 07030, USA

Jossey-Bass, 989 Market Street,
San Francisco, CA 94103-1741, USA

Wiley-VCH Verlag GmbH, Boschstr. 12,
D-69469 Weinheim, Germany

John Wiley & Sons Australia Ltd, 33 Park Road, Milton,
Queensland 4064, Australia

John Wiley & Sons (Asia) Pte Ltd, 2 Clementi Loop #02-01,
Jin Xing Distripark, Singapore 129809

John Wiley & Sons Canada Ltd, 22 Worcester Road,
Etobicoke, Ontario, Canada M9W 1L1

Library of Congress Cataloging-in-Publication Data

Montier, James.
  Behavioural finance : insights into irrational minds and markets / James Montier.
    p. cm. — (Wiley finance series)
  Includes bibliographical references and index.
  ISBN 0-470-84487-6 (alk. paper)
  1. Investments—Psychological aspects. 2. Investments—Decision making. I. Title. II.
Series.

  HG4515.15 .M66 2002
  332.6'01'9—dc21

                                                                    2002027390

British Library Cataloguing in Publication Data

A catalogue record for this book is available from the British Library

ISBN 0-470-84487-6

Typeset by Mathematical Composition Setters Ltd, Salisbury, Wiltshire
Printed and bound in Great Britain by Biddles Ltd, Guildford and King's Lynn
This book is printed on acid-free paper responsibly manufactured from sustainable forestry
in which at least two trees are planted for each one used for paper production.

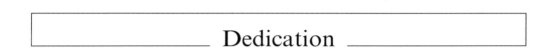

Dedication

To my parents and grandparents

Contents

Preface

To say that economics is a science without behavioural assumptions is to do the dismal science an injustice. From the age of 14, when I first started studying economics, I was introduced to the concept of *Homo Economicus* (HE) or rational man if you prefer. HE is capable of understanding vastly complex puzzles and conducting endless instantaneous optimizations.

When economists talk to their brethren in other social sciences, they have a general tendency to be condescending, assuming that the study of man is a waste of time. As a young graduate economist, I was indoctrinated with this belief. I left university a profound, perhaps even zealous believer in rationality.

This is not a reflection on my tutors, many of whom despaired of my obsession with HE. Rather I was seduced by the elegant beauty and mathematical aesthetics of rationality. However, one lecturer did manage to persuade me to think about the possibility of quasi-rationality and sent me scurrying away to read Richard Thaler's contributions to the *Journal of Economic Perspectives*.

At this time my father was a financial advisor who argued passionately that active management had a role to play in stock markets. There was I, a young brash over-confident economist espousing an efficient markets view of the world of high finance. I am not sure who I feel more sorry for — my father for having to listen to me spout off about such rubbish, or my long-suffering mother who had to endure the debates between Dad and I!

However, after the best part of a decade spent working in financial markets, I've come to the inescapable conclusion that they are anything but efficient. Looking back, the first note I wrote as a young thrusting economist freshly employed at Kleinwort Benson Securities was to set the tone for my education over the next 10 years. I doubt that anyone has ever read my first note, and I can't say that I blame them — it must be one of the few City notes to contain matrix algebra! However, its topic was testing the expectations theory of the term structure — the idea that long-dated government bond yields were simply the rational present value sum of future expected short rates. The article showed that the expectations hypothesis was deeply flawed as a model of the term structure. Long bonds were too volatile.

Old hands around the City used to wisely pontificate over the role of sentiment in driving markets. It is thanks to the efforts of economists and psychologists such as the late Amos Tversky, Daniel Kahneman, Richard Thaler, Meir Statman, Hersh Shefrin,

Robert Shiller and Andrei Shleifer to name but a few that insights from other social sciences are now being incorporated into economics, leading us to an alternative paradigm to the efficient markets hypothesis. It is largely due to the efforts of a generation of young behavioural economists inspired by these pioneers that we are at long last able to quantify the influences of sentiment upon the market. As Newton once said 'If I have seen further [than certain other men] it is by standing upon the shoulders of giants'.

This book is aimed at institutional investors. The work here draws on my own experience in using behavioural finance as a guide to analysing markets. I must thank many of my colleagues — both past and present — for their stimulating discussions, especially Edmond Warner (for constantly forcing me to remember the commercial angle, and teaching me to write), Albert Edwards (who first got me interested in moving from strategy to economics), Leo Doyle and David Owen — whose passion for economics is always enjoyable.

This book wouldn't have been possible without so many of my clients taking a deep interest in the subject. Indeed, much of this book has grown out of a series of lectures that I have given to institutional clients and academic audiences over the last two years. I thank them for lively and insightful questions which have made this work much stronger. Particularly noteworthy are Rupert Cargnie, Katie Pybus and Steve Danby of Hendersons, Alistair Bryne of Aegon and Stephen Barrow of DAM — thank you all.

Special thanks to Christian Elsmark and Richard Taffler provided many useful comments on early drafts of this book. Anne for her support, tolerance and forgiveness during the writing of this work.

Finally, I would like to thank Samantha Whittaker (Publishing Editor) and Carole Millett at Wiley for their help and assistance in bringing this project to completion. As always, this book would not have been possible without input from these and countless others. However, any mistakes and errors are the sole responsibility of the author.

The author and John Wiley & Sons, Ltd have, to the best of their knowledge, obtained or applied for permission to use all material, from copyright sources, reproduced in this book.

Introduction

A man is what he believes

Anton Chekhov

The future belongs to crowds

Don Delillo

Remember Spock? The half human, half Vulcan science officer on the Enterprise. Recall how Spock could never fathom the actions of his emotional colleagues? To the logic-dominated first officer his fully human shipmates seemed to be irremediably illogical, driven by their irrational emotions.

The world of classical finance is populated by Spock and his ilk. Participants in the market are assumed to be totally rational. Fully capable of solving complex dynamic optimization problems in the blink of an eye. But do you also remember how many times Captain Kirk, Bones and Scotty came up with some hair-brained solution that saved the day, much to the bemusement of the half Vulcan logic master, Spock?

This is the world of behavioural finance, a world in which human emotions rule, logic has its place, but markets are moved as much by psychological factors as by information from corporate balance sheets. Those educated in classical finance respond with the claim that the assumptions underpinning their cherished models are irrelevant. That it is the validity of their predictions that should be scrutinized.

Even to sceptics like myself, this seems a reasonable stance, after all if it ain't broke don't fix it. If the models of classical finance work as practical descriptions of the way in which markets function, and can be used as forecasting devices, then there is no need for other approaches.

However, the models of classical finance are fatally flawed. They fail to produce predictions that are even vaguely close to the outcomes we observe in real financial markets. We will show in Chapter 2 that even the most basic tenet of classical finance — arbitrage — is not riskless, as so easily assumed in the traditional approach. Since this is the mechanism by which markets are forced to equilibrate, its absence suggests that markets and their 'fundamentals' can be divorced for long periods of time.

Of course, now we need some understanding of what causes markets to deviate from their fundamental value. The answer quite simply is human behaviour. Psychologists have shown that human decision processes contain several traits that bias our thought process away from a purely rational approach. These traits are shared by almost all of us, creating predictable waves of sentiment in the market place. These traits are explored in depth in Chapter 1.

This raises two further issues, firstly why is the efficient market approach so dominant in academic teaching (especially in the UK), and secondly if the behavioural approach is so successful at explaining the facts why aren't more people making money from it?

On the best courses, the efficient view is taught as a benchmark against which we can measure market imperfections. However, all too often orthodoxies become ingrained, once an idea becomes academic gospel it is very hard to break its strangle hold. Heterodoxies are perceived more as heresies than alternatives, and subsequently attacked by defenders of the orthodoxy rather than evaluated on their merits.

The efficient markets view of the world has the advantage of fitting exceptionally well with an economist's toolkit. Rational agents and optimization problems are economists' bread and butter. The neat, elegant and perhaps even sexy mathematics that accompanies the efficient approach is guaranteed to titillate economists. As Ronald Reagan once remarked 'economists are people who look at reality and wonder if it would work in theory'.

However, whilst in fields like macroeconomics a consensus has begun to emerge around the new Keynesian approach,[1] finance remains a deeply divided subject. This is all the more puzzling since finance is a particularly empirical branch of economics. However, so deep are the ideological chasms between the efficient markets and behavioural approaches that the debate even spills into the normally dry area of econometric methodology (see Chapter 7).

Behavioural finance has witnessed a growing cult of adherents over the last 10–15 years. The late 1990s have witnessed a positive plethora of young bright academics exploring the interaction of psychology, limited arbitrage and financial markets. Increasingly their work has focused on the concerns and issues facing real-world investors.

My friend and colleague, Albert Edwards, has coined the expression 'The Ice Age' to refer to a world in which the return on equities is not massively higher than the return on bonds (see Chapter 6). If this hypothesis is correct (and I firmly believe it is), then fund managers will have to seek alternative methods of adding value. Much of the behavioural finance literature is aimed at explaining the cross-section of returns rather than the time series, i.e. how to outperform (add value) within a time period rather than across time periods. Many of the academic papers cited in this book contain tests formed on the basis of zero net investment portfolios or equal long–short positions

---

[1] It is noteworthy that in macroeconomics the sticky price assumption is usually invoked to create a distortion. John Roberts (of the Federal Reserve Board of Governors) has shown that the data are more closely aligned to a situation characterized by sticky expectations (backward-looking expectations, related to anchoring perhaps) rather than sticky prices (Roberts, 1998). Indeed one of the leading lights of modern macroeconomics — Greg Mankiw — has recently co-authored a paper (Mankiw and Riess, 2001) suggesting some theoretical and empirical advantages of using a bounded rationality approach.

(hedge funds if you prefer). In a low-inflation environment, absolute rather than relative returns are likely to be of prime importance, a shift towards cross-sectional value-added performance seems highly likely. Behavioural finance will help illuminate this path.

As such this leads to the second question, if behavioural finance is so powerful as a paradigm for understanding markets, why aren't more people using it? Efficient marketeers are fond of citing the appalling performance statistics of the active fund management industry, with an average of between 75 and 90% of fund managers underperforming a benchmark index.

Of course, the insightful will have automatically seen that this underperformance isn't an argument in favour of efficient markets. It could (and we believe does) rather reflect the fact that investors simply haven't learnt the lessons offered by behavioural finance. I can speak from personal experience, and say anecdotally that in general, fund management groups around the City are only just becoming deeply interested in the insights offered by the behavioural approach.

PLAN OF THE BOOK

The structure of this book is as follows. Chapters 1 and 2 contain the necessary foundations for understanding the subsequent content. Chapter 1 is a crash course in the psychology of judgement and decision making. It highlights the empirically most consistent findings of psychologists. It also attempts to provide financial applications, so that the practically focused reader can see the immediate benefits available from this approach.

Chapter 2 explores the failure of arbitrage in financial markets. Even in the clearest cases we find the law of one price (identical assets can't sell for different prices bar information and transactions costs) is regularly and blatantly violated. These limits to arbitrage allow irrationality to persist in the market place for prolonged periods of time. Indeed in some models mildly irrational agents actually come to dominate the market.

Once the reader has completed these two chapters, the rest of the book should be largely self-explanatory. Chapter 3 investigates style investing. It explores the issues surrounding value vs. growth and their interaction with momentum, and concludes that understanding style rotation driven by psychological errors is likely to be the optimal approach.

Chapter 4 tackles issues that concern analysts, ranging from valuation techniques and earnings analysis through to constructing cost of capital measures.

Chapter 5 is designed for risk managers and portfolio constructors. It deals with topics such as asymmetric correlations (semi-correlations), estimating the variance–covariance matrix, and explores the limits of risk control via value-at-risk methodologies by showing that market crashes are in fact outliers, rather than extreme events lurking in the fat tails of distributions. Asset allocators will also find this chapter contains some necessary background for the next chapter.

Chapter 6 is dedicated to asset allocation. It explores some of the issues surrounding traditional techniques for both tactical (short-term) and strategic (long-term) selection between bonds and equities. It goes on to show how some behavioural alternatives can enhance the process, such as including data on equity issuance. Finally it examines some findings on predicting financial crashes from the emerging field of phynance (econophysics, if you prefer), using models of structural failure and earthquakes to predict looming stock market crashes.

Chapter 7 deals with issues surrounding corporate finance. Much real-world corporate finance (tracking stocks, carve outs, cycles in equity issuance, etc.) makes little or no sense from the standpoint of classical finance. However, we explore two paradigms associated with the behavioural approach. Firstly we show that models that assume irrational managers but rational markets can explain features such as pecking order capital structure, and the diversification discount. We then switch models to explore a world in which managers are rational but markets are irrational. Using this model we can explore how managers attempt to exploit market inefficiencies in terms of issuing new stock (and of course repurchasing it). The chapter concludes with a plea for work to begin to explore the interaction of irrational managers with irrational markets.

Chapter 8 brings together some of the key measurable variables that those interested in pursuing a behavioural approach should consider tracking.

The reader should pick and choose the chapters that interest her/him most. Below we have outlined some suggested reading orders for various groups of potential readers:

Fund managers: 1, 2, 3, 4, 6, 7
Strategists: 1, 2, 3, 4, 5, 6, 7, 8
Asset allocators: 1, 2, 5, 6, 8
Risk managers/portfolio constructors: 1, 2, 5
Corporate financiers: 1, 2, 7
Analysts: 1, 2, 3, 4, 7

1
Psychological Foundations

Of all the ways of defining man, the worst is the one which makes him out to be a rational animal

Atanole France

It is hard to see how any rational man can ever invest

John Maynard Keynes

1.1 INTRODUCTION

People make mistakes when they invest. There we've said it. That might not strike you as a particularly contentious statement. So let's go further ... not only do investors make mistakes, but they do so in a predictable fashion. At this point, classically trained economists are usually feeling more than a little uncomfortable. However, the simple inescapable truth is that investors don't act like the rational men so beloved by economists.

Humans simply aren't capable of carrying out the dynamic optimization problems required by the tenets of classical finance theory. Instead they use rules of thumb (heuristics) to deal with a deluge of information. In contrast to the Vulcan-like logic of economic man, behavioural finance enlists well-documented psychological traits to replace the rationality assumption.

Of course, like all economists, I have been brought up to judge models not by their assumptions, but rather on the strength of their predictive accuracy. That is an economic model may have assumptions that are patently at odds with reality, however, so long as it predicts the way in which people act, then its assumptions are irrelevant.

Chapter 2 is given over to examples that illustrate that the classical approach to finance is fundamentally flawed. Before we explore these issues, a look at the common behavioural traits is warranted, and hopefully fruitful.

1.2 BIASES OF JUDGEMENT OR PERCEPTION IS REALITY

1.2.1 Over-optimism

Perhaps the best documented of all psychological errors is the tendency to be over-optimistic. People tend to exaggerate their own abilities. Like the children of Lake Woebegone, they are all above average. For instance, when asked if they thought they were good drivers, around 80% of people say yes! Ask a room full of students who thinks they will finish in the top 50% of the class, on average around 80% of them will respond in the affirmative — of course at least 30% of them will be disappointed at the end of the course.

The finding of consistent over-optimism results from a number of psychological biases, such as the illusion of control and self-attribution bias. All too often people are fooled by randomness. People feel they are in control of a situation far more often than they are. Self-attribution bias refers to situations where good outcomes are attributed to skill, whilst bad outcomes are attributed to bad luck. Effectively, 'heads I win, tails it's chance'. Both the illusion of control and self-attribution bias tend to lead people to be overly optimistic.

1.2.2   Over-confidence

Not only are people habitually optimistic but they are over-confident as well. People are surprised more often than they think. The classic study in over-confidence is Lichenstein, Fischoff and Philips (1977). They asked people to answer simple factual questions (e.g. 'Is Quito the capital of Ecuador?') and then asked them to give the probability that their answer was right: subjects tended to overestimate the probability that they were right, over a wide range of questions.

In cases where people are certain they are right, they turned out to be correct only around 80% of the time. In another experiment Lichenstein and Fischoff (1977) gave people market reports on 12 stocks and asked them to predict whether the stocks would rise or fall in a given period. Only 47% of the predictions were correct, but the mean confidence rating was 65%.

Individuals who exhibit over-confidence are said to be not well calibrated. Interestingly, several groups of individuals turn out to be consistently better calibrated, these include professional bookmakers and weathermen! Both groups receive regular feedback following their judgements. Perhaps this represents enforced humility in the face of overwhelming evidence — however, the same conditions don't seem to have inspired such enforced humility in stock market forecasters and analysts!

Over-confidence and optimism are a potent combination. They lead investors to overestimate their knowledge, understate the risk and exaggerate their ability to control the situation. The old adage 'Don't confuse brains and a bull market' springs to mind.

Over-confidence and optimism may well have biological evolutionary roots. Biological studies clearly show that in mating, over-confidence and optimism tend to lead to success (I don't speak from personal experience). It is also worth pointing out that these two traits may well be part of the human condition — in virtually every language, there are five or six times as many optimistic adjectives as pessimistic adjectives.

1.2.2.1   Application: Private Investors

Even with learning only of the existence of these two psychological traits we can already begin to gain insights into the investment process. Most of the work in examining the implications of over-confidence and optimism in individual investors has been carried out by Professor Odean. Below we briefly examine some of his findings.

Odean (1998a) examined data on 10,000 trading accounts at a discount brokerage. He found that individuals who sold a stock and purchased another stock swiftly were acting in a way consistent with that predicted by over-confidence and optimism. The stock the individuals sold outperformed the stock they bought by 3.4% in the first year. When Odean excluded non-speculative trades (liquidity demands, tax loss selling, rebalancing, etc.), he found that the underperformance rose to 5.07%.

Odean (1998b) showed that one of the effects of investors being over-confident was that turnover tended to be high — that is people traded more as a result of being over-confident. Barber and Odean (2000) in an appropriately entitled paper 'Trading is hazardous to your wealth' show that as turnover rises so net profits tended to fall (Figure 1.1).

Psychological studies also show that males tend to be more over-confident and more optimistic than females. The theory suggests that over-confident investors trade excessively. If males are more over-confident, they should trade more excessively than women. Barber and Odean (2001) found that in their sample (Feb 91–Jan 97) men traded 45% more than women (Figure 1.2). Trading reduced men's net returns by over 2.5% per annum, against 1.7% for women (Figure 1.3).

Odean went further, suggesting that some moderation of views and the need to trade would be found in accounts that were owned by couples. That is to say, men would have their over-confidence and optimism muted by their partners. When he took this hypothesis to the data he found that single men traded 67% more than single women, reducing their returns by 3.5 percentage points per year compared to single women. Perhaps single men should find something better to do with their time!

1.2.3 Cognitive Dissonance

Cognitive dissonance is the mental conflict that people experience when they are presented with evidence that their beliefs or assumptions are wrong. People have an incredible degree of self-denial. They will effectively jump through mental hoops in order to reduce or avoid mental inconsistencies.

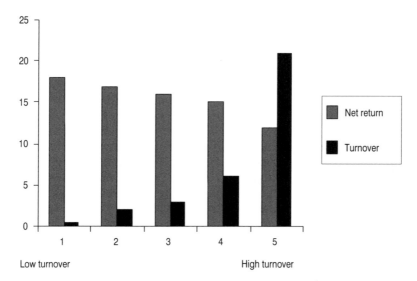

Figure 1.1 Turnover vs. net returns (%)

Source: Barber and Odean (2000). Reproduced from Blackwell Publishers.

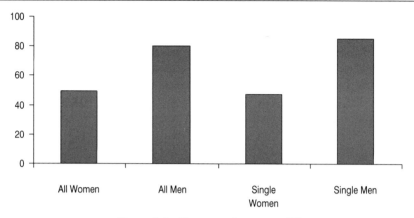

Figure 1.2 Turnover by group (%)

Source: Reproduced from Barber and Odean, The Quarterly Journal of Economics, 116:1 (Feb, 2001), pp. 261–292, Copyright 2001, with permission from MIT Press.

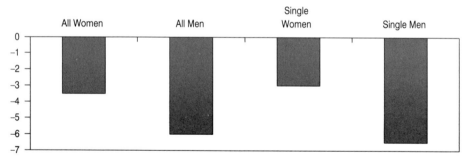

Figure 1.3 Net returns relative to own benchmark by group (%)

Source: Reproduced from Barber and Odean, The Quarterly Journal of Economics, 116:1 (Feb, 2001), pp. 261–292, Copyright 2001, with permission from MIT Press.

1.2.4 Confirmation Bias

Confirmation bias is the technical name for people's desire to find information that agrees with their existing view. Any information that conflicts with the null is ignored, whilst information that reinforces the null is overweighted (also known as self-attribution bias). How often when your view has been challenged by some new data do you say 'never mind it was just a blip'?

1.2.5 Conservatism Bias

This is a tendency to cling tenaciously to a view or a forecast. Once a position has been stated most people find it very hard to move away from that view. When movement does occur it is only very slow (this creates under-reaction to events).

1.2.6 Anchoring

It is well known that when people are asked to form a quantitative assessment their views can be influenced by suggestions. When faced with uncertainty people will grasp at straws in order to find a basis for the view. In an experiment Tversky and Kahneman (1974) asked subjects to answer simple questions such as 'what is the percentage of African nations in the UN?' A wheel of fortune with numbers from 1 to 100 was spun in front of the subjects. Obviously, the number at which the wheel stopped had absolutely no relevance to the question that had been asked. Participants were asked whether their answer was higher or lower than the number shown on the wheel of fortune, and then to give their own answer. The subjects were found to be highly influenced by the wheel of fortune — for example, the median estimates of the percentage of African countries in the UN were 25 and 45 for groups that received 10 and 65 respectively from the wheel.

The value of the stock market is inherently ambiguous. Trying to define fair value is labour beyond even Hercules. In the absence of any solid information, past prices are likely to act as anchors for today's prices. In a clever paper, Statman and Fisher (1998) point out that the Dow Jones Industrial Average (DJIA) excludes dividends — it is a capital index. The DJIA was initiated in 1896 at 40.94 and reached 9181.43 by the end of 1998. However, what would its value be if dividends were included?

When I asked this question at a conference for fund managers the highest guesses doubled or tripled the 1998 level. Statman and Fisher point out that if dividends were included in the calculation of the DJIA then it would have passed 652,230.87 by the end of 1998!

1.2.6.1 Application: Earnings Announcement Drift

The stock market has a tendency to under-react to fundamental information — be it dividend omission, initiation or an earnings report. For instance, in the US in the 60 days following an earnings announcement, stocks with the biggest positive earnings surprise tend to outperform the market by 2%, even after a 4–5% outperformance in the 60 days prior to the announcement (Bernard, 1993) (Figure 1.4). A similar finding is reported by Liu, Strong and Xu (2001) for the UK market.

1.2.6.2 Case Study: Forward Discount Puzzle

One of the puzzles of financial economics (at least from the standpoint of economists) is that some of their most treasured theories simply don't work in the real world. Take foreign exchange markets. When asked to describe the evolution of currencies most economists fall back on either purchasing power parity or the uncovered interest rate parity (UIP).

UIP appeals to the same basic economic laws that we will show to be deeply flawed in Chapter 2. If investors are risk-neutral and have rational expectations, then the market's forecast of the future exchange rate is implicit in the differences in international interest rates. For example, if the UK one year forward interest rate is 7%, and the DM one year forward interest rate is 4%, the interest rate differential is 3%. Sterling must be expected to drop by 3% over the next year otherwise a riskless

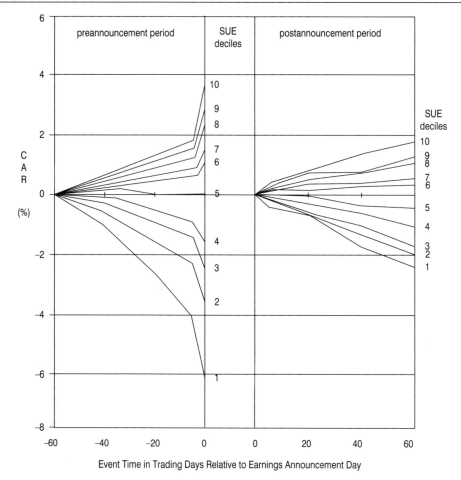

Figure 1.4   Post-earnings announcement drift

Source: Bernard (1993). Reproduced from Russell
Sage Foundation.

profit can be made, by borrowing in DM and buying one year forward pounds
(Figure 1.5).

Anyone familiar with real-world finance (an oxymoron?) will recognize the latter
situation as a carry trade. The fact that carry trades exist shows that despite the size and
liquidity of forex markets, such markets are far from efficient. To test efficiency,
economists frequently run regressions such as:

$$\Delta s = a + b(I - I^*) + e$$

where Δs is the change in the exchange rate, a is a constant, b is the estimated interest
rate effect, $I - I^*$ is the interest rate differential and e is an error term. If UIP is close to
a description of reality then b should equal one. An enormous literature has tested this

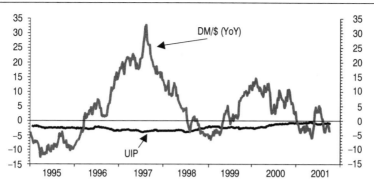

Figure 1.5   UIP — an empirical failure

Data Source: Thomson Datastream.

hypothesis, and found that b is consistently less than one. In fact, b is frequently found to be less than zero! The average coefficient across 75 published studies is -0.9 (Froot, 1990).

A coefficient of close to minus one is hard for economists to explain. It implies that when UK rates exceed foreign rates by one percentage point, sterling tends to appreciate at an annual rate of 1%. Nor is the failure of UIP a sterling phenomenon. As Table 1.1 shows it was possible to make profitable carry trades in many widely traded currency pairs. Note in particular that the coefficient b is negative in all the equations!

Economists tend to give their ignorance a name: risk premia. Classical economists point out that if marginal investors are risk-averse and foreign exchange risk is not fully diversifiable, the interest rate differential reflects not only the expected change in the exchange rate, but also a risk premium. If the assumption of rational expectations is maintained then a finding of $b \neq 1$ means that the risk premium is related to the interest rate. A finding of $b < 1$ implies a 1% increase in the interest rate differential is associated with a less than 1% expected drop in the exchange rate. Since the risk premium is equal to the interest differential less the expected change in exchange rate, this implies that the risk premium must rise with the interest differential.

The consistent empirical finding of $b < 0$ means an increase in the interest differential is associated with a decline in expected depreciation, and therefore an even larger rise in the risk premium. Fama (1984) points out that this implies the variance of the risk

Table 1.1   Profitable carry trades

Against $	DM	£	¥	Sw Fr
Mean appreciation	-1.8	3.6	-5.0	-3.0
Mean differential	-3.9	2.1	-3.7	-5.9
B, 1975–89	-3.1	-2.0	-2.1	-2.6
B, 1976–96	-0.7	-1.8	-2.5	-1.3

Source: Cochrane (1999). Reproduced with permission from The Federal Reserve Bank of Chicago.

premium is greater than the variance of the expected depreciation and the variance of the interest differential. It also implies the covariance between expected depreciation and the risk premium is negative.

A negative correlation between expected depreciation and the risk premium has some appeal — higher inflation might logically be associated with both greater expected depreciation and increased riskiness of holding these assets. The real challenge for believers in the risk premium approach is to explain why a change in interest rates should produce an even larger change in the risk premium. So far no convincing evidence has been presented to account for this relationship.

The alternative to the risk premium approach is that investors have less than rational expectations. Gruen and Gizycki (1993) use anchoring to explain the fact that forward discounts (interest rate differentials) do not properly explain subsequent movements in the exchange rate. They model a situation where at least some investors are slow in responding to changes in interest differentials (they are anchored on the previous number). The other investors are rational, risk-averse and possibly liquidity-constrained. Having these two types of traders generates predictions that match many of the empirically observed elements of the forward discount puzzle.

Such a model yields $b < 0$, as long as changes in nominal interest rates are reflected in some part by changes in real interest rates. If we have anchored traders in the market, not all the changes in interest rate differentials will be immediately reflected in the exchange rate. It takes time for the anchored investors to adjust, hence we may see a negative relationship between short-run changes in interest rates and exchange rates.

A test of the anchored model would be to include past forward discounts in the regression above, effectively incorporating the anchor. If these are added then b should be positive and close to one. Froot (1990) presents evidence that fits with this approach.

1.2.6.3   Application: Anchoring and Valuation

That anchoring can affect valuation (prices) is demonstrated by Northcraft and Neale (1987) in the arena of house prices. All the participants in this experiment were taken to a house for sale, asked to inspect the house for up to 20 minutes, and given a 10-page handout giving information about the house, and about other houses in the area, in terms of square footage, characteristics and prices. The handout given to subjects was identical except with regard to asking prices.

Subjects were asked to give their opinions of the appraisal value, appropriate listing, purchase price and the lowest offer price they personally would accept if they were the seller. The estate agents who were given an asking price of $119,900 had a mean predicted appraisal value of $114,204, listing price of $117,745, purchase price of $111,454 and a lowest acceptable offer price of $111,136.

Estate agents given an initial asking price of $149,900 had a mean appraisal value of $128,754, listing price of $130,981, predicted purchase price of $127,318 and a lowest offer price of $123,818. In effect the initial asking price swayed values by 11–14%!

Working with analysts constantly provides one with examples of anchoring in valuation. For instance, relative valuation — the use of industry average multiples to judge the relative standing of the firm. Stock A looks cheap on a relative PE basis (say) without regard to whether the absolute PE of the industry is 'correct'.

Indeed, I have even heard some analysts when doing discounted cash flow (DCF) valuations look to come up with a number close to the market. Hence the reason that so many fund managers have become highly sceptical of analysts' DCF calculations. Instead of truly working from the bottom up, building a model of 'true' valuation, it is all too easy for analysts to anchor on the current market price — plus or minus 5% say. One way in which to overcome this bias, in the context of analysts' valuations, is to turn the DCF on its head (a so-called reverse engineered DCF). Take the market price and back out what it means for the implied growth of the firm under consideration, then compare with the bottom-up forecasts. However, this approach has yet to find wide acceptance on the sell side — although it should be noted that this does represent a growing trend towards the way in which buy-side researchers tend to work.

1.2.7   Representativeness Heuristic

Remember that heuristics are just rules of thumb for dealing with the information deluge that we are all faced with. Representativeness refers to our tendency to evaluate how likely something is with reference to how closely it resembles something rather than using probabilities.

For instance consider the following:

Linda is 31, single, outspoken and very bright. She majored in philosophy. As a student she was deeply concerned with issues surrounding equality and discrimination.

Is it more likely that Linda is:

A bank clerk

or

A bank clerk and active in the feminist movement?

Most people respond that it is more likely that Linda is a bank teller and active in the feminist movement. This is irrational. We know from simple set theory that the intersection of two sets can never be greater than one of the wholes. Anyone picking the option that Linda is a bank teller and active in the feminist movement is guilty of what statisticians call ignoring the base rates. This is simply ignoring the fact that there are far more bank tellers than there are bank tellers with a side line in activism in the feminist movement — so probability would suggest we go for the first option (Figure 1.6).

One aspect of representativeness is also often referred to as the law of small numbers (mocking the statistical law of large numbers). It is a belief that random samples will resemble each other and the population more closely than statistical sampling theory would predict.

For instance, consider each of the following sequences of coin tossing results from an unbiased coin:

HTHTTH

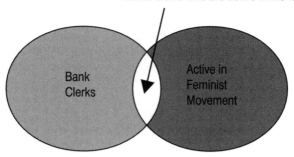

Banks clerks who are active in the feminist movement

Figure 1.6   Venn diagrams

and

HHHTTT

When asked which is more likely many people will say the first, simply because it looks like a random sample. However, of course, both sequences are equally likely (0.5^6). Bloomfield and Hales (2001) have conducted an experiment to see how people react to trying to forecast a random walk. Each subject was given a random walk and asked to forecast the next period. Bloomfield and Hales found two regimes — continuations and reversals. They found that people tended to over-react to changes that were preceded by many continuations, and under-react to changes that were preceded by many reversals.

The representativeness heuristic has many applications in finance. For instance, it seems totally believable that investors are subject to the law of small numbers when dealing with earnings data. If any investor sees many periods of good earnings then the law of small numbers leads him to believe that the firm under scrunity is one with particularly high earnings growth, and hence likely to continue to deliver future high earnings growth. After all, the firm can't be 'average' otherwise its earnings would appear 'average' according to this view. We will use this form of the representativeness heuristic further when we examine the forces governing style investing in Chapter 3.

Another example of representativeness at work is the way in which we often mistake good companies for good stocks (see Solt and Statman, 1989; Shefrin and Statman, 1995). In investors' perceptions a good company is a strong company successful at producing earnings, and earnings in turn lead to higher returns. On the other hand, poor companies are represented by poor earnings, and hence disappointing returns. Investors shun the poor companies, preferring good companies. However, as we will see in Chapter 3, earnings have a habit of mean-reverting, such that 'good companies' are likely to become average, and so are 'poor companies'.

1.2.7.1   Application: Forecast Revisions

One of the accusations levelled at behavioural finance is that at times it predicts over-reaction, and at other times it predicts under-reaction. Fama (1998) claims that under-reaction and over-reaction cancel each other out. So a key challenge for behavioural finance is to explain why we see both under-reaction and over-reaction, and indeed when we should expect to see under-reaction and when we should expect to see over-reaction. Amir and Ganzach (1998) examine changes in earnings and forecasts amongst analysts. They define a change as the difference between future earnings and previously announced earnings, and a revision as the difference between prediction of future earnings and previous forecasts.

The argument is that optimism, representativeness and anchoring all affect analysts' forecasts. Optimism affects both the level of the prediction and its extremity. Overall it leads to overly-optimistic predictions, and when the forecast modification is negative, it also leads to excessively moderate forecasts (under-reaction). Representativeness and anchoring only affect the extremity of the forecast. Representativeness generates excessively extreme forecasts, and anchoring leads to excessively moderate forecasts.

Whether representativeness or anchoring dominates the forecast depends on the salience of the anchor. The more salient the anchor, the greater the likelihood of anchoring dominating. Previous forecasts are more likely to be a salient anchor than previously announced earnings, if only because of the time and work involved in the creation of the forecast in the first place. This is, of course, a sunk cost. Psychologically, people find it hard to forget about such sunk costs, whereas rational agents will ignore sunk costs.

Table 1.2 clearly shows that biases are capable of balancing each other out in certain circumstances, but are equally capable of exacerbating each other as well. There is a greater tendency for anchoring when the analyst's previous forecast is used as the base. This leads to greater under-reaction with regard to forecast revisions (own past forecast) than with regard to forecast changes (previously announced earnings).

Optimism also affects the saliency of the anchor. When positive information is received, analysts are willing to depart from a previous anchor to modify their forecast

Table 1.2   The psychology of forecast revisions

		Forecast errors	Comments
Earnings (*t*)	↑ Over-reaction ↑ Optimism ⊗ Forecast	63% positive 37% negative	On upgrades the biases work in the same direction
	↑ Optimism ⊗ Forecast ↓ Over-reaction	50% positive 50% negative	On downgrades the biases work in opposite directions
Forecast (*t* − 1)	↑ Optimism ⊗ Forecast ↓ Under-reaction	48% positive 52% negative	Balanced bias on upgrades from previous forecast
	↑ Under-reaction ↑ Optimism ⊗ Forecast	75% positive 25% negative	When it comes to adjust previous forecast down, analysts try to minimize the adjustment

Source: Amir and Ganzach (1998).

in a positive fashion. On the other hand, when negative information is processed, analysts are less likely to deviate from an established anchor. There will be more under-reaction (less over-reaction) for a negative forecast modification than a positive one.

1.2.8 Availability Bias

According to Tversky and Kahneman (1974) the availability heuristic is a rule of thumb by which decision makers 'assess the frequency of class or the probability of an event by the ease with which instances or occurrences can be brought to mind'. All else being equal, it isn't a bad rule of thumb — common events come to mind easier than rare events.

However, like all heuristics it can lead us astray. Plous (1993) provides a great example of the availability bias at work:

> 'Which is a more likely cause of death in the United States — being killed by falling airplane parts or by a shark? Most people rate shark attacks as more probable than death from falling airplane parts. Shark attacks certainly receive more publicity than do deaths from falling airplane parts, and they are far easier to imagine (thanks in part to Jaws). Yet the chances of dying from falling airplane parts are thirty times greater than the chances of being killed by a shark.'

Another example comes from Kahneman and Tversky (1973). They asked people the following: 'In a typical sample of text in the English language, is it more likely that a word starts with the letter K or that K is its third letter?'. Of the 152 people in their sample, 105 generally thought that words with the letter in the first position were more probable. However, in reality there are approximately twice as many words with K as the third letter as there are words that begin with K. People index on the first letter, and can recall them easier.

1.2.8.1 Application: Stock Selection

How do you select stocks from the thousands that are available? Some limits are of course imposed on you by the nature of your mandate, off index risk is limited, and liquidity risk is also often closely monitored. However, it may be that your choice of stocks is influenced by the newspapers, or even God forbid by brokers' research.

It is easier for us to recall information that has recently arrived, be it on the front cover of the *FT*, or one of those annoying emails from your pet brokers. Gadarowski (2001) investigated the relationship between stock returns and press coverage. He found that stocks with very high levels of press coverage underperformed in the subsequent two years! Be warned, all that glitters is not gold.

1.2.9 Ambiguity Aversion

People are exceptionally afraid of financial situations involving ambiguity. For instance, in experiments, people are much more willing to bet that a ball drawn at random from a bag containing 100 balls is blue when they know the distribution of balls is 50/50 blue/red than when they only know that the bag contains 100 balls but the distribution between blue and red is unknown.

This translates into extreme caution on the part of investors with regard to stocks they think they don't know. The flip side of the bias is a preference for the known or the familiar.

1.2.9.1   Application: Under-diversification and the Need for Familiarity

Way before Markowitz created modern portfolio theory (MPT) with its sound advice to diversify investment holdings, Shakespeare had written about it:

> 'Oh no, no, no, no, my meaning in saying he is a
> Good man is to have you understand me that he is
> Sufficient. Yet his means are in supposition: he
> Hath an argosy bound to Triplois, another to the
> Indies: I understand moreover, upon the Rialto, he
> Hath a third to Mexico, a fourth to England, and
> Other ventures he hath, squandered aboard. But ships
> Are but boards, sailors are but men: there be land-rats
> And water-rats, water thieves and land thieves, I
> Mean pirates, and then there is the peril of waters,
> Winds and rocks. The man is, notwithstanding,
> Sufficient. Three thousand ducats; I think may
> Take his bond.'

(Shylock. Merchant of Venice, Act I, Scene III)

Just as ambiguity aversion suggests investors are seriously under-diversified, as Table 1.3 shows, the second highest asset allocation amongst 401(k) plans is to company stock!

Benartzi (2000) cites the case of Coca-Cola as an extreme. Coca-Cola employees allocate no less than 76% of their own discretionary contributions to Coca-Cola shares. When asked why in general employees devote so much of their pension to their own company stock the key reason was found to be the past performance of that stock (Figure 1.7).

Of course, the allocation might still be rational — even if it doesn't fit with the tenets of MPT. If the stock continues to do well then the allocation was warranted. Benartzi (2000) tests this hypothesis. He finds that stocks that had relatively low returns in the

Table 1.3   Asset allocation of 401(k) plans (%)

Stock funds	46
Company stock	18
Balanced funds	14
Money market funds	9
Bond funds	8
Stable value funds	3
Lifestyle funds	1
Individual stocks and bonds	1
Other	1

Source: Investment Company Institute.

Figure 1.7   Reasons for investing in employer's stock
Source: ICI.

past had only a 10.4% allocation in 401(k) plans, whereas stocks that had done well in the past had an allocation of nearly 40%. However, he also found that the allocations to company stock were uncorrelated to subsequent returns.

Of course, under-diversification isn't purely the domain of the private investor. There is a massive home bias in international investment. In the US, UK and Japan somewhere between 70 and 90% of the total investment in equities remains at home (Table 1.4).

Why do investors cling to their home country with such vigour? Early suggestions were based around capital controls and information asymmetries. However, these explanations seem less reasonable in today's increasingly integrated world, with global investment banks providing research from and on all corners of the Earth.

Could it be that investors simply prefer to invest in the familiar? Could it be that investors are simply too optimistic about their home market?

Using survey data, Strong and Xu (1999) show that fund managers are consistently more optimistic about their home markets than they are about foreign markets. Table 1.5 shows the average balance of bulls and bears as a percentage of fund managers from October 1995 to October 1999, with investor sentiment covering a one year time horizon. Home markets are represented on the diagonal — so in the US the only group of managers who were consistently bullish were the US-based managers, and the biggest bears were the UK managers.

Table 1.4   Pension funds overseas equities allocations

Country	%
Canada	10.3
Germany	4.5
Japan	9.0
UK	19.7
US	5.7

Source: IMF.

Table 1.5 Over-optimism about 'home'

Equity market	Fund manager			
	US	UK	Europe	Japan
US	7.2	−22.8	−3.2	−8.2
UK	14.8	30.7	20.9	−1.8
Europe	38.2	44.6	57.7	18.4
Japan	26.0	33.6	34.3	49.0

Source: Strong and Xu (1999).

The psychological studies cited above suggest that over-confidence and ambiguity aversion are minimized when people feel in control of a situation and/or are very close to whatever they are being asked about! Fund managers are subject to exactly the same psychological biases and flaws as the rest of us.

Perhaps most bizarrely of all, researchers have unearthed evidence of home bias at home! Coval and Moskowitz (1999) find that one in 10 stocks in a fund manager's portfolio is chosen because it is located in the same city as the manager. In particular, these firms tend to be small, highly leveraged producers of non-tradeable output — suggesting that the closest fund manager feels they may have an informational advantage.

Huberman (1999) examined the geographic distribution of shareholders in Baby Bells. The seven Baby Bells are all listed on the New York Stock Exchange (NYSE), and their market caps are all large — each exceeds $15bn. An investor might wish to hold an overweight position in their local operator as a hedge against unexpected price rises in the services provided. However, given the tiny proportion of expenditure accounted for by telecommunications this would seem unlikely.

An underweight position is more rational. Baby Bells' fortunes are closely tied to their local operating environment. Local investors are likely to be subject to income fluctuations similar to those of their local operator. Hence diversifying into non-local Baby Bells is likely to be the optimal strategy. However, Huberman finds that in all bar one state, more people hold shares in the local Baby Bell than in any other single operator. Yet another blow to the followers of efficient markets!

1.3   ERRORS OF PREFERENCE OR THERE IS NO SUCH THING AS CONTEXT-FREE DECISION MAKING

1.3.1   Narrow Framing

This is also known as frame dependence or mental accounting. Effectively, we are all subject to context sensitivity. We simply don't see through the way in which questions are asked (ask any polling specialist — the way in which you frame the question is pivotal to the answer).

Take the lines below, which is the longer?

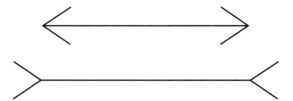

Many people answer that the bottom line is longer. However, when we make the question transparent by adding vertical lines, the true answer that they are both the same length becomes clear:

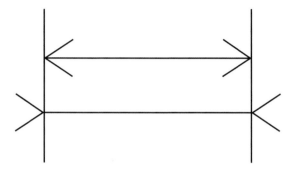

How many of us have separate funds for separate purposes? Holiday money, housekeeping, etc. By creating artificial frames we prevent ourselves from dipping into funds that we want to use for other purposes. Alternatively, do you pay off your credit card balance every month? If not, and you have money in the bank, you are acting irrationally. After all the credit company is charging you 28–29% APR, and your bank balance is earning you a paltry 6% gross if you are exceptionally lucky.

Consider this pair of concurrent decisions:

First choose

(A) a sure gain of £2400

or

(B) a 25% chance of a £10,000 gain and a 75% chance of winning nothing at all.

Then choose

(C) a sure loss of £7500

or

(D) a 75% chance of a £10,000 loss and a 25% chance of losing nothing at all.

When asked these questions most people pick option (A) in the first part. The expected payout for choice (B) is £2500, the extra £100 is not enough to tempt people into taking a chance. With the second question, most people choose (D), they want the chance of avoiding a loss altogether.

However, if you acted in accordance with the precepts of traditional finance theory, you would have maximized expected gains or minimized expected losses and integrated the questions such that:

Options A and D   £2400 − £7500 = −£5100

Options B and C   £2500 − £7500 = −£5000

1.3.1.1 Application: Cash Flows or Earnings?

Investors regularly exhibit frame dependence when dealing with reported earnings. The discount cash flow model of valuation is quite explicit about the determinants of value:

$$\text{DCF Present Value} = \sum [CF_i/(1+r)^i]$$

It is cash flows **not** earnings that investors should be focusing on. Earnings are an amalgamation of cash flows and accruals:

$$\text{Earnings} = \text{Accruals} + \text{Cash Flow}$$

where accruals = (change in current assets − change in cash and cash equivalents) − (change in current liabilities − change in debt included in current liabilities − change in income tax payable) − depreciation and amortization.

Hence by focusing on earnings, investors are failing to see through the way in which cash flows are reported. Sloan (1996) found that a zero net investment portfolio which was long firms with low accruals and short firms with high accruals generated an annual excess profit of over 10%, and generated a positive return in 28 out of 31 years!

Houge and Loughran (2000) update and extend Sloan's study. They find similar results in that regardless of whether the problem is framed in terms of accruals or cash flows, stocks with more cash flow outperform (Table 1.6).

In case you think this is just another representation of the case for investing in value stocks (which tend to be more cash flow generative), Table 1.7 shows the results after we have corrected for both style and size factors (more on this in Chapter 4). As the table clearly shows, the spread between the performance remains essentially unchanged, with the low accruals portfolio outperforming the high accruals portfolio by 8%, and a

Table 1.6 Cash flow vs. accruals — raw returns (% p.a.)

Low accruals	High accruals
18.4%	10.2%
Low cash flow	High cash flow
10.4%	18.6%

Source: Houge and Loughran (2000). Reproduced with permission from Lawrence Erlbaum Associates.

Table 1.7 Cash flow vs. accruals — style-
and size-adjusted returns (% p.a.)

Low accruals	High accruals
2%	−6%
Low cash flow	High cash flow
−6.2%	4%

Source: Houge and Loughran (2000). Reproduced
with permission from Lawrence Erlbaum Associates.

slightly larger result of the high cash flow portfolio outperforming the low cash flow portfolio by 10% p.a.

Houge and Loughran extend Sloan's work to come up with an earnings quality trade. They suggest that firms that deliver low earnings but have a high proportion of cash flows in those earnings are good quality earnings generators. However, firms with high earnings but with a dominance of accruals suggest poor earnings quality. A zero net investment portfolio formed on the basis of buying good earnings quality and selling poor earnings quality yielded an annual average excess return of 16%, and generated a positive return in 23 out of 31 years (Table 1.8).

1.3.1.2   Application Pro Forma vs. GAAP

Investors and analysts alike have allowed themselves to focus on the earnings that the corporates have wanted to report, rather than the earnings that they are forced to report. Montier (2002a) shows that for the S&P500, every $1 of pro forma earnings is worth 47 cents under US GAAP. On a pro forma 8% of the S&P500 companies report losses, on a GAAP basis this rises to 19%. No wonder corporates have been so keen to provide pro forma earnings (Figure 1.8).

This is yet another example of narrow framing. The relationship between GAAP and pro forma can always be examined as follows:

$$GAAP = Pro\ forma + Special\ items + Other\ exclusions$$

New research by Doyle, Lundholm and Soliman (2002) shows that investors could have made significant profits by trading on the difference between pro forma and

Table 1.8 Earnings quality trade construction

	Low earnings	High earnings
Low cash flow	—	Earnings largely composed of accruals, implies poor earnings quality SELL
High cash flow	Earnings dominated by cash flow, implies high earnings quality BUY	—

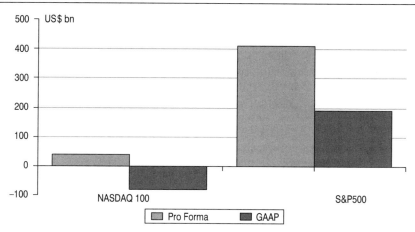

Figure 1.8   Pro forma vs. GAAP: NASDAQ 100 and S&P500 for 2001
Source: DKWR.

GAAP-based earnings. Figure 1.9 shows the potential returns from a zero net investment portfolio structured around the degree of earnings management. The results are hard to ignore. Even on the simplest screen investors could have earned up to 15% over three years (after controlling for size and style). If investors had narrowed their focus to firms that meet or beat analysts' expectations by no more than 2 cents, and where exclusions were greater than surprise (i.e. on a GAAP basis the firm would not have met expectations), the returns were even better — 32% over three years.

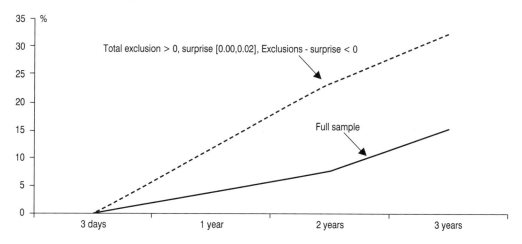

Figure 1.9   Abnormal returns to trading pro forma vs. GAAP
Source: Doyle *et al.* (2002).

1.3.2 Prospect Theory

Prospect theory has probably done more to bring psychology into the heart of economic analysis than any other approach. Many economists still reach for the expected utility theory paradigm when dealing with problems, however, prospect theory has gained much ground in recent years, and now certainly occupies second place on the research agenda for even some mainstream economists. Unlike much psychology, prospect theory has a solid mathematical basis — making it comfortable for economists to play with. However, unlike expected utility theory which concerns itself with how decisions under uncertainty **should** be made (a prescriptive approach), prospect theory concerns itself with how decisions are **actually** made (a descriptive approach).

Prospect theory was created by two psychologists, Kahneman and Tversky, who wanted to build a parsimonious theory to fit a number of violations of classical rationality that they (and others) had uncovered in empirical work. Prospect theory bears more than a passing resemblance to expected utility theory.

Expected utility theory says that the expected utility is the sum of the probability weighted outcomes measured in terms of utility:

$$\Rightarrow \sum p_I u(x_I)$$

Prospect theory assumes people maximize a weighted sum of 'utilities', although the weights are not the same as the true probabilities, and the 'utilities' are determined by a value function rather than a utility function:

$$\Rightarrow \sum \pi(p_I)v(x_I - r)$$

where π is a non-linear weighting function, $v(x - r)$ is the value function evaluated with respect to the reference point — don't worry about these new terms, they will all be explained very shortly.

1.3.2.1 Non-linear Weights

Kahneman and Tversky noted that people tended to give zero weight to relatively unlikely outcomes (but not impossible), and tended to give a weight of one to relatively certain outcomes (but not guaranteed). That is people behave as if extremely unlikely events are impossible and extremely likely events are certain. In general it has been found that people tend to exaggerate the true probability (over-confidence at work).

As Figure 1.10 shows, decision weights tend to overweight small probabilities and large probabilities and underweight moderate probabilities. A typical weighting function lies above the diagonal for low probabilities and high probabilities and below the diagonal for moderate probabilities.

1.3.2.2 Application: Volatility Smiles

Both deep out-of-the-money and deep in-the-money options have prices significantly higher than that predicted by the Black–Scholes option pricing model. This tendency is usually expressed in terms of the implied volatility smile. When the implied volatility for options with various strikes is plotted against the strike price, the curve tends to have the shape of a smile.

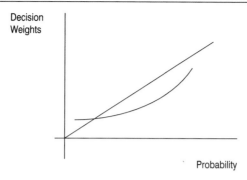

Figure 1.10   Non-linear decision weights

Prospect theory would suggest that people act as if they overestimate the small probability that the price of the underlying stock crosses the strike price, and underestimate the high probability that the price of the underlying stock stays on the same side of the strike price.

1.3.2.3   Value Functions

The other key element of prospect theory is that people value changes not states. Rational man is always assumed to be trying to maximize the (expected) utility of wealth. However, in empirical work one of the inescapable conclusions is that people worry far more about gains and losses than they do about levels.

Figure 1.11 shows a value function — this is prospect theory's equivalent of classical economics' utility function. However, note that it is defined over gains and losses around a reference point (the kink at the origin). The reference point is determined by the subjective feelings of the individual. It is the individual's point of reference, the benchmark (status quo) against which all comparisons are contrasted.

Note in particular that there is a shift in risk attitudes around the reference point (a reflection in mathematical terminology). The value function is concave for gains and convex for losses. This means that the value function is steeper for losses than for gains — this is called loss aversion.

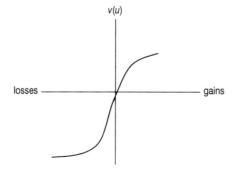

Figure 1.11   A typical value function

Box 1.1   Formal Properties

The value function measures gains relative to a reference point: $v(x - r)$
The value function is concave for gains: $v''(x - r) > 0$ for $x > r$
The value function is convex for losses: $v''(x - r) < 0$ for $x < r$
Loss aversion: $-v(-x) > v(x)$ for $x > 0$

Multiple gains:

$$x > 0, \ y > 0$$

$$v(x) + v(y) > v(x + y)$$

Multiple losses:

$$x < 0, \ y < 0$$

$$v(x) + v(y) < v(x + y)$$

Mixed:

$$x > 0, \ y < 0, \ x + y > 0$$

$$v(x) + v(y) < v(x + y)$$

Consider the following:

You are offered a bet on the toss of a fair coin, if you lose you must pay £100, what is the minimal amount that you need to win in order to make this bet attractive?

The most common answer is somewhere between £200 and £250. That is to say that people feel losses around $2-2\frac{1}{2}$ times more than they feel gains. Indeed I asked this question of some of my colleagues at a previous employer, their responses are shown in Figure 1.12.

Once again the mean answer was around the £200 mark. There were also a considerable number of individuals who required massive compensation in order to take the bet — perhaps they just didn't trust a strategist! It is also interesting to note

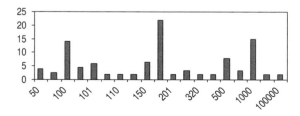

Figure 1.12   Stock brokers' loss aversion

that one of the people who would accept the bet at £50 (i.e. risk-loving) was one of the technology analysts!

1.3.2.4 Application: Equity Risk Premium

In the US, equities have outperformed bonds by around 7% p.a. for most of the 20th century. Economists have long been puzzled by the magnitude of this outperformance. For sure annual stock returns are more volatile than annual bond returns. But most models used by economists show an equity risk premium of 1–2% maximum. Why should stocks require such a large compensation for their risk?

Benartzi and Thaler (1995) propose an explanation based on prospect theory. What if investors aren't risk-averse over variable returns, but rather they care about the chance of a loss. Annual stock returns are negative more often than annual bond returns, and because of this loss-averse investors will require a large premium in order to persuade them to hold stocks.

Bear in mind that the higher annual return to stocks means that the cumulative return to stocks over longer horizons is increasingly likely to be positive as time horizons extend. This is exactly what is observed in the data. Siegel (2000) shows that stocks have never underperformed bonds in the US over a 20 year horizon (Table 1.9).

Therefore to explain the equity risk premium, we need to assume that investors generally have a short time horizon. This is exactly what Benartzi and Thaler call myopic behaviour amongst investors. They compute the prospect values of stocks and bonds over various horizons, using estimates based on experimental data — i.e. assuming loss aversion of 2.25 times, that is that investors feel losses 2.25 times more than they enjoy gains. Benartzi and Thaler show that over a one year time horizon, the prospect values of stocks and bonds are roughly equal if a 7% equity risk premium exists (Figure 1.13).

Effectively, investors with longer time horizons can pick up the 7% equity risk premium as a return for being patient. Perhaps this serves as an insight into the impressive returns that such patient investors as Warren Buffet can generate.

1.3.2.5 Application: The Disposition Effect — Stocks and Houses

Shefrin and Statman (1985) predicted that because people dislike incurring losses much more than they enjoy making gains, and people are willing to gamble in the domain of losses, investors will hold onto stocks that have lost value (relative to the reference

Table 1.9 Stocks for the long run

Holding period	Time period	Stocks outperform bonds (%)
1 Year	1871–1996	59.5
5 Years	1871–1996	72.1
10 Years	1871–1996	82.1
30 Years	1871–1996	100.0

Source: Siegel (2000). Reproduced from McGraw Hill.

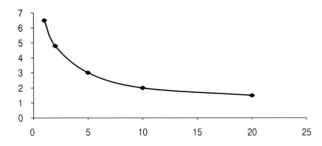

Figure 1.13 Time horizon and ERP

Source: Reproduced from Benartzi and Thaler, The Quarterly Journal of Economics,
110:1 (Feb 1995), pp. 73–92, Copyright 1995, with permission from MIT Press.

point of their purchase) and will be eager to sell stocks that have risen in value. They
called this the disposition effect.

Odean (2001) obtained data from a discount brokerage for around 10,000 accounts.
Each purchase and sale for each account had been recorded. He found that investors
held losing stocks a median of 124 days, and held winning stocks a median of 102 days.
Odean also found that an average of 15% of gains were realized against only 10% of
losses. The only month of the year when this tendency to hold losers was reversed was
in December, when losers tended to be sold for tax loss purposes (Figure 1.14).

Institutional investors frequently dismiss the results of Odean's work as interesting
but not relevant to them. However, remember that prices are largely determined by the
marginal investor, and as such private investors' behaviour matters even if they don't
dominate the market in size.

Investors often claim that they hold losers because they expect them to bounce back
(a fundamental belief in mean-reversion). In Odean's sample the unsold losers returned
only 5% in the subsequent year, whereas the winners that were sold returned 11.6%
after their disposal.

Genesove and Mayer (2001) examine the disposition effect in the Boston downtown
housing market during the 1990s. They find that owners who may be faced with a
nominal loss (negative equity — selling at a price below the one they paid for the
property) tended to set prices too high. Indeed they set prices 25–35% of the difference

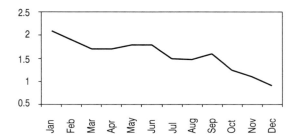

Figure 1.14 The disposition effect

Source: Odean (2001).

between the property's expected selling price and their original purchase price. As a result of setting too high a price, these owners keep their houses too long before selling.

1.3.2.6   Application: Trading — Are Professionals Loss-averse?

Locke and Mann (1999) examine the behaviour of pit traders on the Chicago Mercantile Exchange. The traders they cover work in the following contract markets: $/DM, $/SFr, Live Cattle and Pork Bellies. The study covers these four active contracts over a period of six months. These hardened market pros still sell their winners and ride their losers too far. Once again the traders seemed to suffer loss-aversion, and the disposition effect. Interestingly, when Locke and Mann conditioned their results on performance, they found that the best traders were those who were least loss-averse. That is to say, the best traders sold their losers and rode their winners.

1.3.2.7   Application: VIX

VIX is a weighted average of implied volatilities over four call and four put at-the-money options on the S&P100. As such VIX reflects the consensus of option traders' forecasts for the S&P100 volatility over the next 30 days. To all intents and purposes it is a reflection of the fear and greed amongst a group of market professionals (Figure 1.15).

According to standard finance theory, risk is symmetric — that is a fancy way of saying that upside and downside moves are treated with equal loathing. Personally, I can't think of many fund managers who dislike price rises as much as they dislike price falls (apart from bear funds, of course). Yet symmetry of attitude towards risk is the working assumption of virtually all standard finance. If VIX traders followed the predictions of classical finance then VIX would rise when the index rose sharply and rise when the index fell sharply.

In order to gain insight into the relationship between VIX and contemporaneous market moves, Figure 1.16 plots the percentage change on the month in the S&P100 against the percentage change in VIX. If the predictions of standard finance theory were correct, then gains and losses should provoke exactly the same reaction in VIX traders.

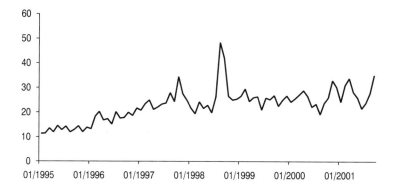

Figure 1.15   VIX chart

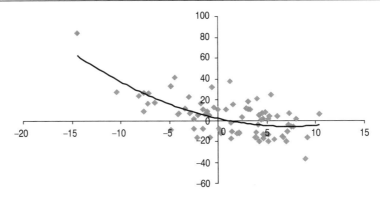

Figure 1.16   Loss-aversion and VIX

However, this is clearly not the case. There is a highly non-linear relationship between moves in the underlying market and VIX traders' pricing. A 5% month on month drop in the S&P100 is associated with a 30% increase in implied volatility. A 5% month on month rise in the S&P100 is associated with a mere 8% decline in implied volatility.

Not only is the relationship downward sloping — losses causing rises in volatility and gains causing declines — but losses have a far greater impact on traded index volatility than gains. This is a direct violation of the predictions of standard finance — but just what prospect theory would forecast.

1.3.2.8   Application: Economics

Finance is far from the only area of economics that can benefit from a healthy dose of irrationality. Indeed, increasingly economists are turning to prospect theory to explore puzzles offered up by traditional models. Camerer (2000) is an excellent short survey on areas of economics where prospect theory has been particularly useful. Table 1.10 shows some examples from Camerer.

1.3.3   Dynamic Prospect Theory

Prospect theory was originally designed to cover one-shot games — i.e. no repeats. However, the theory was later extended to cover decisions in a dynamic context. Critically, for investment analysis, the perception of risk changes dependent upon prior outcomes.

Thaler and Johnson (1990) investigated how people's attitudes to risk changed over sequential gambles. They found that people were more willing to take a gamble if they had previously won money than if they had lost money. Thaler and Johnson interpreted this as revealing that losses are less painful if they occur after prior gains, and more painful if they occur after prior losses. The result of their experiment was to show that risk tolerance went down after prior gains. This is also known as the house money effect — after the fact that gamblers seem more willing to bet money they have won

Table 1.10 Applications of prospect theory to economics

Domain	Phenomenon	Description	References
Labour economics	Downward sloping labour supply curve	NYC cabdrivers quit around daily income target	Camerer *et al.* (1997)
Consumer goods	Asymmetric price elasticities	Purchases more sensitive to price increases than to cuts	Hardie, Johnson and Fader (1993)
Macro-economics	Insensitivity to bad income news	Consumers don't cut consumption after bad income news	Shea (1995), Bowman, Minehart and Rabin (1999)
Consumer choice	Status quo bias	Consumers do not switch health plans, chose default insurance	Samuelson and Zeckhauser (1988), Johnson *et al.* (1993)

Source: Reproduced with permission from 'Prospect theory in the wild', C. Camerer (2000) by Cambridge University Press.

already (i.e. the house's money) than if they started the evening on a losing streak (Figure 1.17).

1.3.3.1 Application: Implied Equity Risk Premium and TAA

Dynamic prospect theory looks highly useable. It clearly shows that risk perceptions change dependent upon prior returns. Put into a market context — when a stock or market has done well, investors charge less for accepting the risk. This tallies exactly with what we observe when we back out an implied equity premium from the market.

I tend to use a very simple method for deriving the implied equity risk premium. I take the current dividend yield on the market plus the long-term growth rate (generally nominal GDP growth) minus the current 10 year bond yield. It isn't sophisticated in any sense, but it does give a quick and dirty sense as to where in the investors' risk tolerance cycle we are.

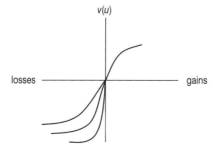

Figure 1.17 Shifting value functions

Figure 1.18   Implied equity risk premium
Data Source: Thomson Datastream.

As a check I construct a 'bottom-up' implied equity risk premium (ERP) by doing the same calculation as above, but replacing the nominal GDP growth rate with the product of the current payout ratio multiplied by the long-term earnings growth forecast from bottom-up analysts (from I/B/E/S).

As you can see from Figure 1.18, the implied ERP does drop during long bull markets during which investors build up a store of gains, and then it starts to rise as prices start to drop, slowly but surely eroding the gains in the store. Indeed, if you had been watching this measure you might even have spotted the peak of the US market in early 2000 — when the implied equity risk premium reached the same lows it did in 1987!

1.4   CONCLUSIONS

This chapter serves as a brief introduction to the psychological biases that plague investors. If you are anything like me, then a lot of these biases will ring all too true. The high priests of market efficiency say that whilst all of this is interesting it is irrelevant — efficient markets don't require all participants to be rational. Instead, they require only that some are rational, and they will drive the rest out of business. Plus, as many of these biases suggest over-reaction, and others suggest under-reaction, efficient market zealots tell us that they cancel each other out. As we will see in the next chapter, psychological biases do affect prices, and to such an extent to make arbitrage a risky business for the hyper-rational amongst us.

2
Imperfect Markets and Limited Arbitrage

Traditional Finance is more concerned with checking that two 8 oz bottles of ketchup is close to the price of one 16 oz bottle, than in understanding the price of the 16 oz bottle

Larry Summers

To make a parrot into a learned financial economist it needs to learn just one word — arbitrage

Stephen Ross

The market can stay irrational longer than you can stay solvent

John Maynard Keynes

It were not best that we should all think alike: it is the difference of opinion that makes horse races

Mark Twain

2.1   INTRODUCTION

At the very heart of the standard approach to finance is the assumption that arbitrage is riskless — that the market mechanism will always correct mispricing by smart rational investors. The assumption of 'no arbitrage' (i.e. all profitable arbitrage has been carried out) is embodied in just about every aspect of standard financial theory, from option pricing to corporate capital structure. However, as we have shown in the previous chapter, investors as a whole can and do make mistakes. Those mistakes are not the random blips of efficient markets, but rather persistent, pervasive and at least to some extent predictable outcomes of psychological biases inherent in investors.

Economists are fond of trotting out the law of one price (LOOP). This says that identical goods must have identical prices. For example, an ounce of silver should have the same price (expressed in pounds) in London as it does in New York. If this were not the case then silver would flow from one city to the other. Of course, LOOP could only be expected to hold in perfectly competitive markets with no transaction costs and no barriers to trade. Students of international trade spend a great deal of their time studying the imperfections that can and do prevent LOOP from holding in their markets. However, finance students are frequently informed that low transaction costs and low barriers to entry ensure that LOOP is a good assumption when dealing with financial markets.

However, as we have already shown, LOOP is not a good description of financial markets. In the case study on the forward discount puzzle in the previous chapter we showed that LOOP simply didn't describe the way in which foreign exchange prices move. This chapter will explore other examples of the violation of LOOP, and also explore the impact of these violations on the assumption of riskless arbitrage.

Table 2.1   Failure of LOOP in the ketchup market

Grams	Price (p)	Relative weight	Price based on LOOP	% Mispricing
1140	155	3.33	197	27
885	125	2.59	153	22
570	69	1.67	98	43
342	59	1.00	59	0

2.2   KETCHUP ECONOMICS

Before investigating breakdowns of LOOP in financial markets, let's return to Larry Summer's quote above. He went on to say that 'They have shown that two quart bottles of ketchup invariably sell for twice as much as one quart bottle of ketchup except for deviations traceable to transaction costs ... Indeed, most ketchup economists regard the efficiency of the ketchup market as the best established fact in empirical economics'.

A quick check on the internet site of a well-known UK supermarket revealed the following pricing structure for a leading brand of ketchup. A 342 g bottle of ketchup was priced at 59p, and a 570 g bottle cost 69p. These prices violate the LOOP, since ketchup is being sold at 1.72p per 10 g in the smaller bottle and 1.21p per 10 g in the larger bottle. Relative to the 342 g bottle, the 570 g bottle should sell for 98p, so the actual price represents a mispricing of 43%! (See Table 2.1.)

Two questions spring to mind: Why don't arbitrageurs correct the mispricing by selling the overpriced bottle (342 g) and buying the underpriced bottle (570 g)? And even if there is something that stops the arbitrageurs, why would anyone ever buy the overpriced bottle (342 g)?

Of course, the retail ketchup market is not a liquid market. It is hard to envisage how arbitrageurs could exploit the mispricing (at least not without getting very messy!). There is also no way of hedging the position. Say you go long in the cheap bottle (570 g), how do you construct the other side of the position, a short in the expensive bottle (342 g) — after all the supermarket certainly isn't about to start buying small bottles of ketchup from you.

As to why anyone buys the expensive bottle — it presumably comes down to preferences. For some reason consumers prefer having small bottles of ketchup, perhaps they look good on the dining room table, perhaps storage space is at a premium in the fridge.

2.3   EFFICIENCY AND LOOP

Fama (1991) defines an efficient market as one in which 'deviations from the extreme version of the efficiency hypothesis are within information and transactions costs'. The ketchup market outlined above, according to the Fama criterion would be classed as an efficient market — although it contains a 43% mispricing!

Financial markets are likely to be considerably easier to conduct arbitrage in — after all transaction costs are not massive and short sales are generally possible. Some of the mispricings we will outline below are so massive that given the probable level of transaction costs they must imply financial market inefficiency.

Testing LOOP is easier than testing market efficiency. In order to test market efficiency, a model of the correct or fundamental value of the market is required. Fama (1991) calls the problem of testing market efficiency the 'joint hypothesis' problem — 'market efficiency per se is not testable. It must be tested jointly with some model of equilibrium, an asset pricing model'. When testing LOOP no notion of fundamental value is required — we don't need a model of asset pricing to know that identical assets should have identical prices.

2.4   STOCK MARKET

My own career has largely been spent in the equity market, and it is here we will begin our investigation into violations of the LOOP in financial markets. It is also the market in which the most flagrant violations of LOOP occur (for reasons we will explain later).

2.4.1   Twin Securities

Remember it is fundamental to classical finance that one asset cannot sell at different prices bar transaction and information costs. The most obvious example of violations of the LOOP in equity markets comes from so-called twin securities. These are stocks that are listed on more than one exchange, creating an obvious opportunity for arbitrageurs to keep prices in line with LOOP.

Perhaps the best known example of a twin security is Royal Dutch Shell. Royal Dutch and Shell are separate legal entities and are independently incorporated. However, in 1907 they signed a charter agreeing to merge their interests on a 60:40 basis. Cash flows adjusted for tax and control rights are effectively split in this proportion. If we assume that equities should be valued on the basis of cash flows, and the market is efficient, then the market value of Royal Dutch should be 1.5 times greater than the market value of Shell (currency adjusted).

So tradeable are Royal Dutch and Shell that they are listed on no less than nine exchanges. Indeed both of them are listed on the US and Amsterdam exchanges. In general however, Royal Dutch trades primarily in the US and the Netherlands, and Shell trades predominately in the UK.

Figure 2.1 shows the deviations from the theoretical parity. They are massive — swings from −30% to +20%. No level of transaction costs in the developed financial markets can account for these swings.

Unilever N.V. and Unilever PLC stand out as another example of twin securities that regularly breach the LOOP price by significant amounts. Unilever N.V. and Unilever PLC are once again independently incorporated firms. In 1930, they established an agreement to equalize cash flows. The agreement was designed to bring the two companies together as a single entity as far as possible. They even share the same board of directors. The equalization agreement states the distributions are 'made on the basis that the sum paid as dividends on every 1 pound nominal amount of PLC capital is equal ... to the sum paid as dividends on every 12fl. nominal of ordinary capital of N.V.'. PLC shares are listed as 5 pence per share, and N.V. shares are listed at 4fl. per

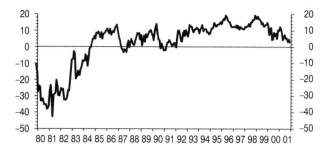

Figure 2.1   Royal Dutch Shell — deviations from theoretical parity
Data Source: Thomson Datastream.

share. Thus earnings per share are equated by (1/5) PLC EPS = (12/4) N.V. EPS (in a common currency). (See Figure 2.2.)

Unilever trades on eight exchanges. N.V. trades mostly in the Netherlands, Switzerland and the US. PLC shares trade mainly in the UK. As with Royal Dutch Shell, the relative pricing of Unilever PLC and N.V. pays scant regard to the price according to LOOP, with deviations ranging from −50% to 0%.

Royal Dutch Shell and Unilever are not alone (see Froot and Dabora, 1999). There are many other twin securities, all of which exhibit the same magnitude of deviations from the LOOP theoretical price — SmithKline Beecham and Daimler Chrysler stand out amongst the offenders.

Why don't arbitrageurs move in more swiftly to close these valuation anomalies? The answer lies in what behavioural economists call noise trader risk. Let's say you put on the Royal Dutch Shell trade at a level of −10%, say, then some of the market's less rational participants drive the spread out to −25%. All of a sudden you are facing massive margin calls, and you are beginning to doubt your own sanity (let alone rationality) in putting the trade on in the first place! The real problem for arbitrageurs in situations like these is that there is no well-defined end point — no guaranteed

Figure 2.2   Unilever PLC vs. N.V.
Data Source: Thomson Datastream.

closure if you like. There is nothing to force the two shares back into LOOP's 'implied equilibrium'.

So we now know why it is that arbitrageurs don't always rush in to exploit the mispricing of twin securities. But why would anyone want to buy the expensive share? One potential explanation lies in the nature of the investment process itself.

Royal Dutch is part of the S&P500, whereas Shell isn't. Given that in recent years, Royal Dutch has traded at a premium to the LOOP price, there must exist a class of investors who for some reason are perfectly willing to hold the overvalued share — they are of course the index funds. Their mandate is 'simply' to track the index — so relative valuation anomalies have no part in their world. We will return to the role and impact of index funds a little later.

2.4.2 Equity Carve Outs

An equity carve out occurs when an existing firm decides to float a specified part of itself. These have become increasingly common in recent years — a fact we will return to in Chapter 7 on corporate finance. Thaler and Lamont (2000) examine equity carve outs in the high tech sector between 1995 and 2000, and find overwhelming evidence of widespread market mispricing.

The highest profile case they examine is that of 3Com/Palm. On 2/3/2000, 3Com sold a fraction of its stake in Palm via an initial public offering (IPO). 3Com retained some 95% of the shares, and announced that pending IRS approval, it would spin off the remaining shares before the end of the year. 3Com investors would receive about 1.5 shares of Palm for every 3Com share they owned.

For example, investors could buy 150 shares of Palm directly, or 100 shares of 3Com — giving an entitlement to 150 shares of Palm plus a share of 3Com's other assets. Since the price of an equity can never be less than zero, the law of one price creates a simple inequality: the price of 3Com must be at least 1.5 times greater than the price of Palm.

The day before the Palm IPO, 3Com closed at $104.13. After the first day of trading, Palm closed at $95.06, implying a 3Com price of at least $145.59. In reality 3Com's share price actually fell to $81.81. Effectively the market was pricing 3Com's non-Palm assets at −$60.78 (what economists call a negative stub value). Analysts were saying that 3Com's non-Palm business was probably around $35 per share, and with cash and securities on the balance sheet equivalent to $10 per share, a negative stub value certainly indicates a flagrant breach of the LOOP.

This situation wasn't a state secret, the *Wall Street Journal* ran a story on the day after the Palm float pointing out the potential arbitrage situation. However, as Figure 2.3 shows, the negative stub value attached to 3Com persisted for over two months! So much for the speedy dispersion of information in assets markets.

Unlike the twin securities problem, in the case of equity carve outs there is usually a good chance of closure. For instance, with 3Com/Palm, 3Com announced it was seeking IRS approval for total disposal, ahead of the IPO. Somewhere around 500 similar spin outs had already been approved by the IRS, so it seems unlikely that arbitrageurs were overtly concerned about the IRS rejecting the proposal.

However, arbitrageurs found shorting the cost difficult in general — as most of it was in the hands of private investors. Even when stock could be borrowed, it was

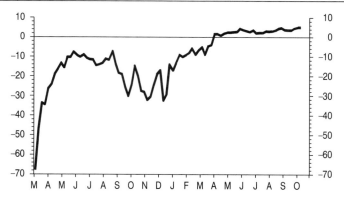

Figure 2.3   3Com/Palm — negative stub value

Data Source: Thomson Datastream.

expensive to do so. Thaler and Lamont show in detail the costs imposed on arbitrageurs who were tempted to short Palm.

Just as with the ketchup market this answers the first of the two questions that any breach of LOOP should stimulate — why don't arbitrageurs correct the mispricing? However, so far we have said nothing about the second question, why would anyone buy the overpriced asset (Palm)?

Just as with ketchup, the only feasible answer is that some investors have odd preferences — they are irrational and want to hold Palm regardless of its relative overvaluation. 3Com/Palm is not alone. Thaler and Lamont find six out of the 18 carve outs they studied between 1995 and 2000 had similar outcomes. Interestingly, Thaler and Lamont show that their sample clusters heavily around the year 2000, suggesting that investor demand for certain types of stocks was unusually high. We now know this period as the internet bubble, of course. It should serve as a timely reminder that sentiment matters just as much if not more than fundamentals for prices in equity markets.

There is one law of economics that does hold even when the law of one price is violated — the law of supply and demand. As Thaler and Lamont conclude:

'Prices are set where the number of shares demanded equals the number of shares supplied. In the case of Palm, some investors were willing to pay ridiculous amounts in order to get the shares, and the supply of shares to sell could not rise to meet that demand because of short sale constraints. Similarly, if some investors are willing to bid up the shares of Internet stocks, and not enough courageous investors are willing to meet that demand by selling short, then optimists will set the price.'

2.4.3   Parent Company Puzzle

The parent company puzzle is related to both the twin securities and the equity carve out detailed above. It refers to a situation where the market value of a company is less than the sum of its publicly traded parts. For example, Figure 2.4 shows the relationship between the market value of Fayrewood (a UK listed stock) and its 51%

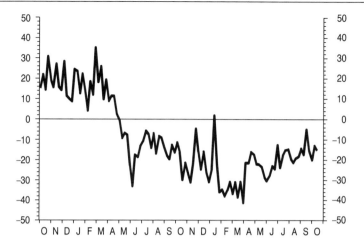

Figure 2.4   Fayrewood and Computerlinks — deviations from parity

Data Source: Thomson Datastream.

shareholding in Computerlinks (a Neurer market listed stock). As can clearly be seen, Fayrewood is valued at less than the market value of its holding in Computerlinks. Of course, there could be some major off balance sheet liability that makes this perfectly rational (say if we were talking about a tobacco stock with cancer liabilities), but that simply isn't the case here.

It shouldn't be thought that this kind of situation merely affects small companies. Few would doubt that General Motors (GM) is amongst the largest companies in the world — with a market capitalization of $256bn. However, GM had tracking stock[1] for one of its subsidiaries — Huges Electronics. GM also held a 20% stake in the publicly listed firm Commerce One.

Both Huges and Commerce One were active in the exceedingly desirable sectors of Technology Media and Telecommunications (TMT). The rest of GM devoted itself to a finance company and, of course, building cars. Between September 1999 and January 2000, Huges' stock price rose 97%, and Commerce One's stock price rocketed by 413%. According to industry analysts, in March 2000, GM's $75 per share included around $60 per share from Huges and Commerce One, leaving GM's core businesses valued at just $15 per share, or a 1.5 × PE ratio! Although the stub value of GM was not negative, few would doubt that this is a sizeable violation of LOOP.

Cornell and Liu (2000) examine seven cases where the parent company puzzle holds (Table 2.2). The only explanation they can find is that the demand curve for stocks slopes down. In particular they note that this is magnified in the case of the subsidiary because the share of the float available to the public is usually only small. The size of the parent's holding means that a small change in the public's desire to hold the subsidiary leads to a large change in the stock price.

---

[1] Tracking stock is a separate share of equity with the rights to the cash flow generated by a specific entity within the parent company.

Table 2.2   The parent company puzzle

Parent	Subsidiary	Time period	Max % held by parent	Daily trading volume (parent)	Daily trading volume (subsidiary)	R^2
Cordant Technologies	Howmeat International	12/97–05/00	84.6	149,020	54,501	0.1132
Flowers Industries	Keebler Foods	01/98–	55	405,311	231,893	0.0385
The Limited, Inc.	Intimate Brand	01/97–	84	935,122	465,351	0.6876
IPC Communications	Ixnet Inc.	08/99–06/00	73	42,891	406,601	0.4330
Medical Manager	Careinsite	06/99–	72	466,474	186,950	0.5010
3Com	Palm	03/00–	94.8	6,750,000	5,110,000	0.5312
Seagate	Veritas	05/99–	41.6	2,320,000	5,700,000	0.4310

Source: Cornell and Liu (2000).

To test how easy it would be to arbitrage this anomaly, Cornell and Liu regress the subsidiary returns on the parent returns and market returns — they find low R^2 in general suggesting difficulties in constructing appropriate hedges, despite the size of the parent's holding. This helps to explain why the mispricing isn't corrected by the market — the costs of arbitrage are simply too high. However, it remains a puzzle why anyone would buy the expensive asset. The only conclusion must be that the demand curves for these stocks slope downwards.

Mitchell, Pulvino and Stafford (2001) examine no less than 70 such situations between 1985 and 2000 (Table 2.3). They show that no less than 26% of these situations

Table 2.3   Convergence — perhaps

Event	Number of occurrences	Mispricing eliminated	Mispricing not eliminated
Parent distributes subsidiary shares to parent holders	12	12	0
Third party acquires subsidiary	13	5	8
Parent acquires the % of subsidiary that it doesn't already own	5	3	2
Third party acquires both parent and subsidiary	7	4	3
Third party acquires parent	2	1	1
Subsidiary acquires parent	2	2	0
Parent stock is delisted	8	4	4
Both parent and subsidiary are delisted	2	2	0
Parent and subsidiary stock prices change eliminating mispricing	15	15	0
Mispricings not eliminated as of 31/12/00	4	—	—
Total	**70**	**48**	**18**

Figure 2.5   Discount to NAV — UK closed end funds
Data Source: Thomson Datastream.

terminate without convergence! This lack of convergence happens when there is a corporate event that permanently alters the relative mispricing in a fashion that damages arbitrageurs' positions. Mitchell, Pulvino and Stafford find the most common failure to converge is a third party paying a takeover premium to acquire the subsidiary firm. Given that an arbitrageur's position requires they be short in the 'expensive' subsidiary it is clear to see how such a takeover could do them untold damage. So much for riskless arbitrage.

2.4.4   Closed End Funds

Closed end funds (investment trusts) are portfolios of assets, controlled by a management company, which trade as listed securities. Figure 2.5 shows the average discount of net asset value (NAV) (the underlying asset value) for UK general listed closed end funds. The figure clearly shows that the price of the fund and its NAV can depart company for prolonged periods of time.

This is not quite a pure example of a violation of LOOP. One reason that the two values may diverge lies in agency costs. The portfolio manager of the fund charges a fee for her service and incurs other expenses, thus the cash flow to the holders of the fund is different from the cash flow to the holders of the underlying assets. However, as Shleifer (2000) shows, the deviations of actual price from NAV are simply too great to be accounted for by agency issues, tax liabilities or underlying illiquidity problems. Effectively, the persistent and varying discount attached to closed end funds is yet another example of a violation of the LOOP.

2.5   OTHER MARKETS

Lest it be thought that it is just the equity market that violates LOOP, the fixed income and foreign exchange markets are also capable of illustrating the failure of one of economists' most deeply cherished ideals. We have already shown the gross violations of LOOP exhibited by the foreign exchange markets in our case study in the previous chapter (see p. 7). We turn now to LOOP indecencies exposed in the other financial markets. Interestingly, most of the research in the fixed income arena phrases its discussions in terms of 'completeness' rather than efficiency or violations of LOOP, however, they amount to one and the same thing.

2.5.1 Callable Bonds

In theory, callable bonds should be worth less than the equivalent non-callable bond because they contain an embedded option that can only hurt the bond holder, i.e. the right to call the bond back in. Longstaff (1992) found that some callable bonds were worth more than the equivalent portfolios of non-callable bonds. The degree of mispricing found by Longstaff was 1.26% — trivial by the standards we have observed in the equity markets but still troubling.

2.5.2 Liquidity Premium

Longstaff (2001) examines whether there is a flight-to-liquidity premium in Treasury bond prices by comparing them with prices of bonds issued by Refcorp, a US government agency (Figure 2.6). Refcorp is unique amongst US government agencies in as much as their principal is fully collateralized by Treasury bonds, and full payment coupons are guaranteed by the Treasury.

Since Refcorp bonds are, in effect, guaranteed by the Treasury, they have the same credit as Treasury bonds. Longstaff finds a large liquidity premium in Treasury bonds,

Figure 2.6 Refcorp — Treasury spread and liquidity premium

which can be more than 15% of the value of some Treasury bonds. He also finds strong evidence that this liquidity premium is related to changes in consumer confidence, flows into equity and money market mutual funds, and changes in foreign ownership of Treasury debt. This suggests that the popularity of Treasury bonds directly affects their value.

2.5.3 Strips

Strips are zero coupon bonds created from either the principal or the coupons of individual bonds. Stripping is generally motivated by the desire of investors to match future liabilities with a zero coupon asset. If the maturity date and face value are identical, then the cash flows from a strip derived from a principal are identical to the cash flows from a coupon-derived strip.

Daves and Ehrhardt (1993) show that LOOP is regularly violated in the strip market. They find a mean difference of 1.2% in terms of price between principal- and coupon-derived strips. They also find price differentials as large as 2.7% on a regular basis.

However, strips based on principal and strips based on coupons differ with respect to both liquidity and their role in the reconstitution of a bond. Just as a strip is created by separating principal and coupon payments, so it may be rebuilt along the same lines. Principal strips have a special role to play in the reconstitution process. In order to reconstitute a bond it is necessary to purchase a series of single coupon strips with maturities and payments corresponding to each of the original payment dates, however, they do not need to have been derived from the original bond. They can come from any bond as long as the coupon payments match the original dates. In contrast the principal strip must come from the original bond.

Daves and Ehrhardt suggest that the costs of arbitraging principal and coupon strips are too high to make profits. However, some group of investors must for some reason prefer to hold principal strips — presumably once again this is a liquidity demand.

2.5.4 Bills vs. Bonds

Amihud and Mendelson (1991) and Kamara (1994) both find significant differences between the prices of highly liquid T-bills and older, less liquid T-bonds with no remaining intermediate coupon payments and identical maturity dates. These conditions ensure that the examined bonds are subject to an exact law of one price relationship, as opposed to the more usual on/off the run trade where there is an element of fundamental risk — albeit miniscule — from the fact that the bonds have different maturities. In the case in point the securities are producing identical cash flows in every state of the world — matching Scholes' definition. However, the studies above find that older, less liquid T-bonds have a significant premium compared to newer, more liquid T-bills. Indeed the premium accounts for some 10% of the older T-bond yields.

2.5.5 On/Off the Run Trades

This is perhaps the most infamous of all fixed income arbitrage trades, made so by the demise of Long Term Capital Management (LTCM). The trade involves shorting the

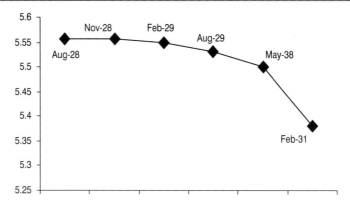

Figure 2.7   Long end yield curve

freshly issued on-the-run long bond, and hedging with the previous on-the-run bond —
now called the off-the-run bond. Figure 2.7 shows the long bond yield curve.

As you can see, there is a high premium attached to the freshly issued bond (some
12 bps in the figure). However, the spread between the previous on-the-run bond and
the previous off-the-run bond is a mere 3 bps. This suggests an obvious convergence
trade, short the newly issued bond, at a spread of 12 bps to the old bond, purchase the
old bond, hold the position until the next auction date (in six months' time), and then
unwind the position at the smaller spread of 3 bps.

In order to establish the short position, the arbitrageur must borrow the newly issued
on-the-run bond in the repo market. In doing so the arbitrageur receives interest at the
repo rate on his short sale proceeds. The repo rate is, of course, market driven, so if the
demand for borrowing a new bond is particularly high, the repo rate will fall below
other market interest rates.

This is known as specialness in fixed income parlance. Specialness means that an
owner of the new on-the-run bond can lend these bonds in the market and earn an
additional return equal to the difference between the overnight rates and the repo rates.
For an arbitrageur holding the convergence trade, a low repo rate on a newly issued
bond translates into a non-negligible carry cost.

Krishnamurthy (2001) investigates this convergence trade closely. He finds that the
average profit is close to zero despite the fact that convergence occurs. He concludes
that simply committing capital for a long period of time is not enough, in order to make
the trade profitable some ability to time the market is required. When sub-samples are
investigated it transpires that betting on convergence was a profitable strategy prior to
the Fall of 1998, however post that period it is no longer viable.

2.6   IMPERFECT SUBSTITUTES

So far we have been considering the case where the market has perfect substitutes. This
removes the 'fundamental risk' from arbitrageurs — that is they are market-neutral.
However, most arbitrage opportunities don't involve perfect substitutes.

Scholes (1972) defined a close substitute as an asset with similar cash flows in all states of the world to the cash flows of the underlying asset. This closeness is vital for arbitrage, because it creates more than one way of achieving a given pattern of cash flows in different states of the world. Scholes reasoned that individual stocks must have close substitutes in order for arbitrage to work well. If this were the case then arbitrageurs could sell expensive stocks and buy cheap close substitute cash flows instead.

However, given the violations of LOOP outlined above dealing with perfect substitutes, what chance have imperfect substitutes got? Roll (1988) showed that the amount of variation in returns for large stocks explained by aggregate economic factors, the contemporaneous return on other stocks in the same sector and public firm-specific news was just 35% on monthly data and a mere 25% on daily data! Put another way there is very little substitutability between equities, less than a quarter of the daily volatility of a typical equity can be hedged away.

2.6.1 Index Inclusion and Demand Curves for Equities

If arbitrage works then the demand curve for equities should be flat (perfectly elastic). Non-news about non-events shouldn't impact upon prices. Starting with the seminal work by Shleifer (1986) the addition and deletion of stocks from an index has proved a fertile ground for testing the assumption of perfectly elastic equity demand curves.

When a stock is removed from an index, it is simultaneously replaced by another. Indices are frequently constructed based on such criteria as size, trading volume/liquidity or industry classification, etc. All of these factors are public information, and none of them contains any information about the future prospects and performance of the stock.

As index funds are mandated to track the relevant benchmark, they have little choice but to buy equities that enter the index. As such their buying represents an outward shift in the demand curve for the stock entering the index, and it is unrelated to any good or new information about the stock. If the demand curve for the stock was horizontal, inclusion in an index should not be accompanied by any price increase. After all the holders of the stock should be willing to sell to the index trackers, and buy a similar claim on cash flows at a cheaper price.

However, this is not what we observe. Instead, index inclusion creates swirling masses of interest, and has significant price effects. As Table 2.4 shows, the mean announcement day abnormal return has been steadily rising over time, as indeed has the incidence of such effects.

Wurgler and Zhuravakaya (1999) go one stage further in their analysis of the price effects of index inclusion. They point out that stocks with exceptionally poor substitutability will have even larger price effects stemming from index inclusion. They show that stocks with little in the way of available substitutes experience about 1.5 percentage point higher price effects than stocks with reasonable substitutes when entering an index.

Kaul, Mehrata and Morck (2000) point out that an obvious event with which to examine the slope of demand curves for stocks is one that changes supply. In the absence of new information, a shift in the supply curve should not affect stock prices if demand curves are flat (Figure 2.8).

Table 2.4 Announcement day returns for stock additions to the S&P500

Period	No. of additions	Mean announcement day abnormal return	Percent of abnormal returns > 0
1976–1980	42	2.32	85
1981–1985	76	2.70	91
1986–1990	84	4.25	99
1991–1996	34	4.87	100

Source: Wurgler and Zhuravakaya (1999).

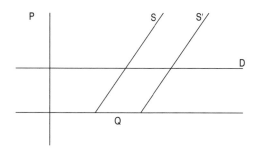

Figure 2.8 Tracing a demand curve when supply shifts

Of course, in order to test this hypothesis we need to find an event that alters the supply of an equity without containing any information at all. Kaul, Mehrata and Morck use index adjustments on the Toronto Stock Exchange (TSE). In November 1996, the TSE redefined the public float for listed firms to include all ownership stakes of less than 20%, up from 15% previously. This decision increased the index weights of 31 stocks, however, it contained no news or information about the future performance of these stocks.

Kaul, Mehrata and Morck find that the affected stocks experienced abnormal returns of 2.3% during the event week. Indeed no price reversal was observed even when trading volumes returned to normal levels. This is a clear indication that the demand curve for stocks slopes down.

*Aspiring PhD students interested in this field might like to look and see if the recent changes to a free float methodology by such leading index suppliers as FTSE and MSCI has similar effects.

2.7 LIMITED ARBITRAGE

According to the assumptions of classical finance, arbitrage is carried out by individual traders all taking small positions using their own capital. Under these assumptions, the greater the deviation of prices from fundamentals, the more aggressively arbitrage will be carried out, as the potential return is at its highest.

However, as we have seen repeatedly, both the transactional and informational costs of arbitrage are non-trivial. For instance consider the market for stock borrowing (see D'Avolio, 2001 and Geczy, Musto and Reed, 2001). In a typical equity loan, the borrower delivers cash collateral of 102% of the market value of the stock he wishes to borrow to the lender. The lender will then typically invest with cash collateral at market interest rates (usually the Fed Funds rate), and then rebates some of this interest. In the US, equities fall into two categories for borrowing purposes. Most stocks are within the general collateral (GC) group. These stocks are easy to borrow due to an excess supply, and generally have low fees of between 10 and 25 bps (high rebate rates 75–90%). In marked contrast some stocks are special. These stocks are hard to find and D'Avolio found an average fee of 3.2% (although the maximum was 82%!) (low rebate rates on average of 50%).

Special stocks have the additional problem that their supply constraint is likely to be binding. That is if the stock is borrowed, but in short supply, and the lender wants the stock back, then the arbitrageur will find it exceptionally difficult to replace the stock from another lender. Indeed D'Avolio finds that 17 out of the 20 most expensive stocks are recalled at some point in his sample. In the wider context of this sample, 19% of all specials were recalled.

D'Avolio investigates the determinants of stock specialness. He finds that specials are more likely to be small stocks with low institutional ownership and high levels of difference of opinion regarding fundamental valuation.

Empirically, he finds that IPOs, momentum losers and glamour stocks are all much more likely to be specials — and hence have very high costs associated with trying to short them. Geczy, Musto and Reed confirm many of these findings (Figure 2.9). They find that an average IPO starts with a rebate rate of 3.2%, which declines to 1% over the subsequent six months. They also find that growth stocks are five times more expensive to short than value stocks, and three times more expensive to short than average stocks!

Arbitrageurs are forced to operate in complex markets where value is uncertain and correct hedges elusive. In fact the risks facing arbitrageurs can be broken down into:

I. Fundamental risk
II. Financing risk/noise trader risk
  - Horizon risk
  - Margin risk
  - Short covering risk

Let's examine each of these in turn.

2.7.1 Fundamental Risk

This is simply the risk that the arbitrageur may be wrong about the position they put on. This is most obvious when we are dealing with imperfect substitutes. For instance, say you are an arbitrageur and you go long stock A and short stock B, because you perceive a relative mispricing. In fact stock A then releases some good news that justifies its higher rating relative to stock B, the arbitrage position must be closed, and at a loss.

There is also fundamental risk in many of the cases we have examined when discussing the failure of LOOP. For instance, what would have happened to the

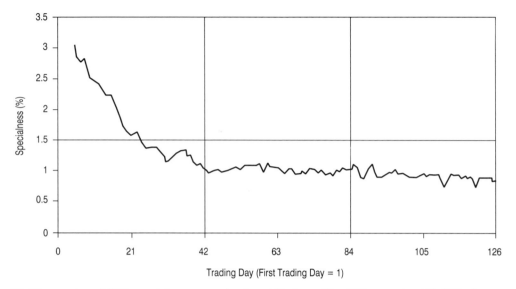

(1) Time series of IPO specialness over the first 180 days. The IPOs are the 110 IPOs in our sample which were covered by our equity-loan data out to their 126th trading days. The figure for trading day *n* is the average specialness of all IPOs in the panel that were loaned on their respective *n*th trading days.

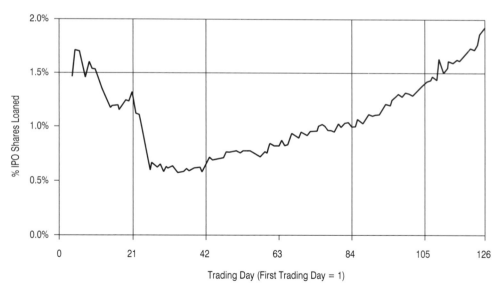

(2) Time series of IPO shares loaned by our data provider, as a fraction of IPO shares issued. The IPOs are the 110 IPOs in our sample which were covered by our equity-loan data out to their 126th trading days. The figure for day *n* is the average of (Loaned Shares)/(Shares Offered at IPO) across all IPOs in the panel on their respective *n*th days, including the IPOs that were not loaned on day *n*.

Figure 2.9 IPO special fee

Source: Geczy, Musto and Reed (2001).

3Com/Palm situation if the IRS had not approved the spin off. In the case of the parent company puzzle in general, Mitchell, Pulvino and Stafford (2001) point out that fundamental risk is akin to the occurrence of an event that terminates the trade before convergence. That is to say, in their sample no less than 25% of the negative stub value trades examined closed without converging, most of these caused by a third party taking over either the parent or the subsidiary.

2.7.2 Financing/Noise Trader Risk

This group of risks reflects the fact that arbitrageurs know they are irrational noise traders in the market, and hence there is always the risk that the position may get worse purely because of the noise traders — as an arbitrageur you face uncertainty over the resale value of the assets that form your position. We can break these risks down into three separate components to help make them transparent.

2.7.2.1 Horizon Risk

Even if prices are guaranteed to converge, they are not obliged to do so in a timely or indeed a smooth manner. Increasing the length of the path to convergence lowers the arbitrageur's return. In the case of the parent company puzzle this is certainly a non-trivial issue. The minimum time horizon in the Mitchell, Pulvino and Stafford data is 1 day, the median 92 days and the maximum 2796 days.

Mitchell, Pulvino and Stafford offer the following numerical example. To see how the time horizon affects returns consider an investment expected to generate 15% over 92 trading days. This represents an annualized return of 47%. A decrease in the number of days until termination from 92 days to 46 days increases the annualized return to 238%. On the other hand, if we extend the time to converging termination to 138 days, the annualized return drops to a mere 14%.

2.7.2.2 Margin Risk

This is perhaps the best known and understood of the risks facing arbitrageurs. When a position moves against the arbitrageur, he is more than likely to face a margin call — a demand for a certain level of partial payment in the face of the new value of the securities he is dealing in.

In the presence of noise traders (irrational investors) it should be clear that this is a significant handicap to arbitrageurs. If a position moves against them, just when the potential returns are increasing they find themselves having to reduce their exposure in order to meet the margin payment.

In fact, Longstaff and Liu (2001) show that in markets where arbitrage is possible but risky, the optimal strategy for an arbitrageur is to take a smaller than maximum position, allowing himself room for potential margin calls.

2.7.2.3 Short Covering Risk

The third element of financing risk concerns the risk of involuntary liquidation. In the discussion below we will investigate the role of principal–agent problems in arbitrage.

However, for now we are referring to a situation whereby an arbitrageur borrows stock to short. When the available free float is small, stock lenders may find it difficult to maintain the level of supply to the arbitrageur. When the owner of a stock demands that the loaned out stock be returned, the arbitrageurs have no choice but to liquidate their position prematurely.

2.7.3 Principal–Agent Problems and Arbitrage

On the basis that the assumptions on the ability to arbitrage so glibly made by classical finance simply don't hold, we need to question the other assumptions about market structure. Remember, classical finance says arbitrageurs are small, numerous and use their own capital. How does this match up with the structure of the professional arbitrage markets?

In reality, of course, arbitrage is the province of a relatively small number of highly specialized investors. Not only that but they don't invest (just) their own money but rather they act as managers running funds for others.

It has long been recognized in other areas of economics that the separation between principals and agents can affect market dynamics. In a world of specialized arbitrageurs running other people's money, we can observe a clear separation of information and capital provision. This point was first made in a seminal work by Shleifer and Vishny (1997).[2] This separation has three important implications for arbitrage.

Firstly, the outside investors (the capital providers) are ignorant about the nature of the trades and markets that the arbitrageurs are working in. They find it difficult to tell good arbitrageurs from bad arbitrageurs. Because these capital providers are risk-averse, they will limit the amount of cash they provide to the arbitrageurs. Effectively, the arbitrageurs are capital-constrained.

Secondly, because the capital providers are poorly informed about the operations of the arbitrageurs, they tend to use past performance to gauge the ability of the arbitrageur, and then allocate funds on this basis. So an arbitrage fund that has done well in the past will have few problems in gaining access to new funds, however a fund that has done poorly in the past will find itself struggling to raise finance.

Thirdly, the arbitrageur's information is highly specialized, and hence they tend to operate only in the spheres of their knowledge — markets are segmented. Foreign exchange arbitrageurs tend to stick to the forex market, bond arbitrageurs stick to the fixed income market, and so forth.

These implications are especially important in extreme circumstances. It transpires that arbitrage under the structure we have outlined above will be at its least powerful just when it is needed most. When prices and fundamental values are at their widest divergence the ability of the arbitrageurs to act is at its most limited. At this point of widest divergence, the potential returns to arbitrage are also at their widest. The informed and knowledgeable arbitrageurs know this, but the capital providers don't necessarily understand this process. In fact, from their position, they may have

---

[2] Shleifer and Vishny effectively outlined the fate that awaited perhaps the most famous hedge fund of all — LTCM — five years before the events that took place in 1998; although the final paper wasn't published until 1997 it was circulating in draft form from at least 1995.

witnessed a string of negative returns from their investment, as the arbitrageur put the position on, and then the market moved in the opposite way (due to noise trader risk) producing negative returns. If capital providers are assessing the arbitrageurs on the basis of past performance, this negative return will lead them to question their investment, and possibly even seek to withdraw funds. Even if this is the extreme case, it will be hard to persuade investors to stump up cash in the face of negative returns.

Anyone who doubts the accuracy of this situation is advised to read Dunbar (2000). He tells of the difficulty that LTCM faced when they tried to raise more capital in the face of negative returns. This difficulty was encountered despite less than a year earlier forcibly returning some $2.7bn to investors in the fund, because the principals felt the fund was becoming too unwieldy.

The arbitrageur's situation deteriorates if he is funded by debt rather than equity. The value of the securities held by the arbitrageur is collateral for the loans. However, if due to either fundamental risk or noise trader risk the position moves against the arbitrageur, the value of securities will decline. This represents an erosion of the arbitrageur's capital base, so leverage rises but borrowing ability falls.

These situations limit the desire of arbitrageurs to get involved in markets to the fullest extent possible. Arbitrageurs face the risk of involuntary liquidation because of the withdrawal of funds, creating the possibility of asset fire sales. An asset fire sale describes the situation whereby arbitrageurs are forced to liquidate their positions at a time when the best potential buyers (other arbitrageurs) have limited resources, and moreover the influx of new external capital is severely limited. Under these conditions, prices fall way below the level justified by the fundamentals.

The risk of involuntary liquidation helps to explain why arbitrageurs are more prevalent and active in some markets than others. At first it may appear that arbitrageurs would be attracted to relatively volatile markets, after all such market turbulence should create large amounts of mispricing to be exploited.

However, arbitrageurs actually seek to minimize the total risk they are exposed to. The easiest way of doing this is to focus on markets without high levels of fundamental risk. For instance, fair value in the bond market is relatively easy to compute, after all the periodic payments (interest) that investors receive is defined at the outset. In contrast, there is much larger fundamental risk in the equity markets where true fundamental value is pretty much anyone's guess.

Arbitrageurs are also generally specialist. This focused style of investing means that they are not particularly well diversified. Even if a high level of diversification is achieved, the correlation between markets has an unhelpful habit of increasing as markets fall — just when that diversification is most needed it disappears.

In many ways, this lack of diversification is yet another hallmark of the LTCM affair. The major theme underlying virtually every trade implemented by LTCM was an overwhelming belief in convergence. LTCM was relatively well diversified by hedge fund standards in terms of its asset distribution — both across asset classes and geographically. That is to say LTM dabbled in equities as well as bonds, and was active in a wide variety of markets from the US and the UK to Japan and beyond. However, the strategy suffered a terminal blow when Russia defaulted in 1998. A panic spread through markets, and petrified investors headed for safe havens. This systemic aversion to risk literally brought LTCM to its knees. None of their convergence trades were immune — all the asset classes in all the countries they were covering suddenly experienced massive divergence, and LTCM was left with the painful realization that it was an unhedged (and probably unhedgeable) risk.

Interestingly, during the early rounds of margin calls that LTCM was forced to meet, a discussion at the head office centred on which positions to sell in order to meet these margin calls. According to Lowenstein (2001), LTCM chose to sell its least profitable positions first. This, as we now know, was yet another error. The least profitable positions were in highly illiquid markets. As these positions were sold they created gyrations that only exacerbated the flight to quality — making even their profitable trades unprofitable. Interestingly, Scholes argued against this strategy, saying that they should sell the most profitable trades first. If they had followed his advice the story might just have been very different.

2.8   POSITIVE FEEDBACK TRADING

So far we have concentrated on situations where the arbitrageur knows about the mispricing but is unwilling to actively seek to push the correction as hard as he could for fear of unpredictable behaviour by noise traders. However, if noise traders aren't random (and the traits detailed in Chapter 1 are relatively universal) then the situation changes.

Freidman (1953) argued that speculators must be stabilizing, since investors who acted in a destabilizing fashion would on average lose money, and hence be eliminated from the market. However, if a market contains noise traders and they aren't random in their actions then it may be rational for arbitrageurs to exploit them.

Specifically, if noise traders follow positive feedback rules then arbitrageurs can exploit them and in the process become destabilizing (see De Long *et al.*, 1990). Positive feedback investors buy stocks after they have gone up and sell them after they have gone down. Effectively they exhibit trend-chasing behaviour.

De Long *et al.* quote Andreassen and Kraus as evidence that people can and do follow positive feedback trading rules. Andreassen and Kraus showed authentic share price charts to subjects with some training in economics. Subjects were given an initial endowment and asked to trade with every new observation in the price series. They were told that their decisions couldn't affect the price. When, over some period of observation, the level of the stock price didn't change much relative to the period-by-period variability, the subjects tended to track the average price level. They sold when the price rose, and bought when it fell. However, if prices began to exhibit a trend relative to period-by-period variability, investors began to chase the trend — buying when prices rose, and selling when they fell. As noted in Chapter 1, Bloomfield and Hales (2001) found that their subjects tended to over-react to sequences of trend behaviour when predicting random walks.

If arbitrageurs know about this behaviour they can exploit it. Indeed George Soros claims to do just that. In his book, *The Alchemy of Finance*, he describes one such situation in the 1960s. Soros noted that a number of poorly informed investors were getting excited about the earnings being generated by conglomerates. Soros argues that the best strategy under these circumstances was not to short the conglomerates and wait for a correction (a strategy that wouldn't have paid off until 1970 incidentally), but rather to buy conglomerate stocks in expectation that other poorly informed investors would continue to enter the market. De Long *et al.* show the market dynamics for an environment with positive feedback noise traders ... the results look incredibly like stock market bubbles. More on that in Chapter 5.

2.9 RISK MANAGEMENT AND LIMITED ARBITRAGE

A new generation of models by theorists such as Kyle and Xiong (2001), Gromb and Vayanos (2001) and Danielsson, Shin and Zigrand (2001) have begun to model situations where arbitrageurs face wealth constraints. These theoretically very rigorous papers have vital implications for risk management processes.

Traditional risk management processes tend to implicitly assume that the statistical relationship governing asset prices (in terms of returns, covariances and correlations) is exogenous, and can be estimated from historical data. However, as hopefully has become clear by now, this is not a sound assumption. Trading patterns can and do impinge upon market prices. The fact that arbitrageurs face risks in taking positions ensures this.

To see the potential problems one only has to think about the LTCM crisis once again. Remember, LTCM was not unique, many of the firms with which LTCM did business held very similar positions. So once market gyrations occurred, they were amplified because all the risk management systems across many firms flashed the same danger signals. This, of course, led to everyone heading for the exit at the same time, driving market prices far below the levels that the risk management systems could ever have envisaged. Risk managers need to devote time to building models that allow the endogeneity of returns, covariances and correlations. Behavioural finance suggests some ways in which this may be possible, and we will explore asymmetric correlations, semi-variances and the distribution of asset returns in Chapter 5.

2.10 ON THE SURVIVAL OF NOISE TRADERS

The standard view offered up by economists is that irrational traders would get wiped out in the long run, as they consistently lose money. However, as we have shown above both limited arbitrage and positive feedback situations suggest that noise traders could exist for sustained periods of time.

In order to really assess the possibility of long run noise trader risk we need to understand a little biology. At the heart of biology lies the concept of evolution — descent with modification if you like. Evolutionary biology has a number of analogies with finance, for instance see Table 2.5 adapted from Doyne Farmer (2000).

Early attempts to study the survival of noise traders, such as De Long et al. (1990), studied the wealth accumulation process for investors assuming that the risky asset was infinitely elastic, and that returns were exogenously given. Under these assumptions investors' beliefs affect their demand for the risky asset but not the price. Essentially what happens in these models is that the noise traders are over-optimistic and over-confident, resulting in an overestimation of returns and an underestimation of risk. The combination outcome of these expectations is that noise traders hold more than they should of the risky asset, but end up with the reward for doing so — i.e. the classical finance outcome that more risk equals more return accrues to the noise traders, and they survive on that basis.

Hirschleifer and Luo (2001) suggest that over-confident investors buy and sell more aggressively in response to private signals, and end up exploiting liquidity traders more

Table 2.5 Evolution, ecology and finance

Biological ecology	Financial ecology
Species	Trading strategy
Individual organism	Trader
Genotype	Functional representation of an investment strategy
Phenotype	Actions of the strategy (when to buy and sell)
Population	Capital
Animals	Speculators/arbitrageurs
Selection	Capital allocation
Mutation and recombination	Creation of new strategies

Source: Adapted from Doyne Farmer (2000).

profitably than rational investors would have done. In an imperfectly competitive stock market, over-confident traders can benefit from intimidating competing informed traders (Kyle and Wang, 1997).

However, the most powerful arguments for the long run survival of noise traders come from Wang (2001). Wang uses evolutionary game theory to study the population dynamics of a securities market. In his model, the growth rate of wealth accumulation drives the evolutionary process, and is endogenously determined. He finds that neither under-confident investors nor bearish sentiment can survive in the market. Massively over-confident or bullish investors are also incapable of long run survival. However, investors who are moderately over-confident or bullish can survive. In fact these moderately over-confident investors can actually come to dominate the market if fundamental risk is sufficiently large.

Think about Wang's findings in the light of the TMT bubble. Those who have lost most are the bears, who have had to tolerate years of miserable performance, and the massive bulls who predicted that tech stocks could never go down. Indeed, it is the pessimistic fund managers that have lost mandates, and the overly bullish private investor who has been wiped out — evolutionary theory at its best. The best performers during the tech boom are those who rode the bubble up, and then sold out shortly after the market had turned down ... the moderately over-confident investors.

Classical finance is yet again at fault for assuming that irrationality cannot persist in the long run. Furthermore, as Keynes pointed out 'In the long run we are all dead'.

2.11 INFORMATIONAL IMPERFECTIONS

Financial markets are also prone to informational imperfections. The textbook image of a financial market is one in which information is instantaneously digested and analysed, and prices adjusted accordingly. Were it true of course, I would be out of a job; thankfully the financial markets are not supercomputers at processing information.

2.11.1 The Sorry Tale of the Cure for Cancer

This example, taken from Huberman and Regev (2001), is a prime case of where a 'non-event' had a major market impact. On Sunday 3 May 1998, the *New York Times* carried an article on a potential new cancer drug being researched by EntreMed. EntreMed's stock price rose to $85 from a close on the previous Friday of just over $12. The stock subsequently fell back during trading on Monday 4 May to close a very respectable $52. Three weeks later the stock price was still above $30.

Fine you may say, surely that was the market incorporating new information. But that is exactly the point at which we hit a problem. This wasn't new information. The potential breakthrough had been reported no less than five months earlier in *Nature*, and in numerous popular newspapers including the *New York Times*! Enthusiastic public attention induced a permanent rise in EntreMed's share price, even though no genuinely new information had been given to the market.

2.11.2   Massively Confused Investors Making Conspicuously Ignorant Choices

The above title comes from a wonderful paper by Rashes (2001). He examines the co-movement of stocks with similar ticker symbols. Ticker symbol confusion is found to lead to interesting price movements in stocks for which there is no new information introduced to the market.

The title of Rashes' paper concerns one of the principal cases he examines, MCI and MCIC. MCI Communications (MCIC) is one of the largest telecommunications companies in the world. From the end of 1996 through 1997, it was engaged in merger negotiations with several companies, before eventually being acquired by Worldcom. Until the acquisition, it traded on NASDAQ with the ticker MCIC. Massmutual Corporate Investors is a closed end fund that trades on NYSE under the ticker MCI. The fund invests most of its assets in long-term corporate debt and converts. In spite of the fact that MCI and MCIC have nothing to do with each other, there is an unusual degree of co-movement between the two stocks. Between November 1 1996 and November 13 1997, of the 24 days during which 10,000 or more shares of MCI changed hands, 18 are days on or immediately prior to significant announcements relating to MCIC merger plans! The simple fact is that investors consistently make mistakes.

Rational asset pricing theories don't preclude investors from making mistakes. However, they should of course be corrected by arbitrageurs ... some chance! Making occasional mistakes doesn't preclude rationality per se, however Rashes goes on to document another five cases in which ticker confusion has caused some truly bizarre market movements. As Rashes notes 'If this trivial group of noise traders can persistently impact the price of MCI, one could only imagine what would occur if a group of correlated noise traders experienced a change in sentiment regarding a group of stocks'.

2.11.3   Dot.coms and Name Changes

Our final example of bizarre informational inefficiency is drawn from an entertaining study by Cooper, Dimitrov and Rau (2001). They study firms that change their names to include some mention of dot.com. Across their sample of firms drawn from AMEX, NYSE and NASDAQ between June 1 1998 and July 31 1999, Cooper, Dimitrov and Rau find that in the five days surrounding the announcement of a name change to incorporate dot.com into the corporate title, an abnormal return of 53% is generated. Even in the [+1,+60] event window an abnormal return of 23% is generated. See Table 2.6.

Table 2.6 Abnormal returns for firms changing their names

Firm	Event window	
	[−2,+2]	[+1,+60]
All	53%	23%
Pure internet firms	36%	59%
Change of name to better reflect nature of business (some prior internet business)	105%	−31%
Refocusing purely on internet business	14%	−2%
Firms whose core business is non-internet	23%	140%

Source: Cooper, Dimitrov and Rau (2001).

Perhaps most bizarrely of all, Cooper, Dimitrov and Rau find that firms whose core business is unrelated to the internet, but who nevertheless decide to alter their name to include a dot.com reference, generate a 23% abnormal return in the five days surrounding the announcement, and even worse a 140% abnormal return in the [+1, +60] event window. A prime example of the representativeness heuristic at work. So much for markets being able to process information efficiently.

2.12 CONCLUSIONS

In this chapter we have demonstrated that some of the assumptions made by classical finance theory, whilst seemingly innocuous, are in fact dangerously at odds with the way in which financial markets actually work. One of the most fundamental laws of economics, the law of one price, is regularly violated in equity, bond and foreign exchange markets.

Arbitrageurs have a tough time trying to correct the mispricings, because arbitrage is far from costless, let alone riskless. We have shown that when transaction costs, informational costs and fundamental and financing risks are considered a much closer approximation to real-world financial markets is achieved. This is further supplemented by a better understanding of the overall structure of the arbitrage market place.

We have also covered two other key areas. Firstly, we have suggested that when noise trader behaviour is predictable (and Chapter 1 shows that the mistakes people make tend to be fairly universal), then arbitrageurs may actually become destabilizing ... exacerbating the mispricing rather than correcting it. We have also discussed the fact that, contrary to standard beliefs, noise traders, or irrational market participants, cannot only survive into the long run, but may under certain circumstances actually come to dominate the market place.

In the rest of this book, we will use the psychological biases outlined in Chapter 1, and the limited arbitrage framework of Chapter 2 to explore a number of important issues in finance including stock valuation, tactical asset allocation and corporate finance.

3
Style Investing

3.1 INTRODUCTION

Before we even start to discuss style investing, it is worth while pointing out that in order to do so, we are stepping outside the realms of classical finance. Classical finance tells us that every security we could want to investigate is fully and perfectly described by just two numbers, the mean and the variance. Talking about style means moving beyond the framework offered by classical finance. In fact style investing can be seen as a form of mental accounting. We are giving securities an arbitrary label, in order to separate them from each other.

Style investing is increasingly popular amongst institutional investors. Indeed, some buy-side houses define themselves with respect to the style of investing they conduct. The battle ground between the so-called value managers and the growth managers is a very bloody one, littered with the corpses of failed strategies. As we will see from this chapter, wedding oneself to a particular style is likely to be sub-optimal. In fact style rotation holds the key to maximizing returns.

3.2 THE DATA

In general, we will follow industry standards in our definition of value and growth. Major index providers such as MSCI have created value and growth indices. These are usually simply formed on the basis of the universe of stocks being ranked by price to book, and then split into two equal market capitalization groups. The top half of the index (high price to book) is given the title of growth, whilst the bottom half of the index is defined as value.

These indices are far from perfect. However, the gains to more precise definitions are murky. Fama and French (1998) show that on a variety of different measures, the essential conclusions that we outline below are upheld. For the sake of replication, we will generally use the MSCI data.

3.3 THE HISTORY

As Figure 3.1 clearly shows, value has outperformed growth in the long run. At the global level, value has outperformed by 3.2% p.a. (1975–2000). Before value managers jump up and down proclaiming victory it should also be noted, as the figure also makes

Figure 3.1   Global value vs. growth

Data Source: Thomson Datastream.

Table 3.1   Value vs. growth around the world (1975–2000)

Country	Value	Growth	Difference
US	16.1	15.3	0.8
Japan	12.5	6.5	6.0
Germany	14.7	13.0	1.7
France	21.0	16.0	4.0
Italy	22.25	20.25	2.0
World	16.0	13.0	3.0

Data Source: MSCI, Thomson Datastream.

Table 3.2   The percentage of years in which value exceeds growth total returns

Country	%
World	64
US	58
Japan	76
Germany	66
France	64
Italy	48

immediately clear, that there have been distinct and relatively prolonged periods of growth stock outperformance (Table 3.1).

In fact in the US on an annual basis, value exceeds growth only around 60% of the time, that is less than two thirds of the time. This pattern is repeated in virtually all the major global equity markets. Only in Japan does a significantly higher value triumph rate emerge, at around 76% of the time (Table 3.2).

3.4   POTENTIAL GAINS TO STYLE ROTATION

The potential gains to timing these switches in style are significant. For instance, Table 3.3 shows the potential gains from picking the best performing asset class/equity style as opposed to a static mix (buy and hold). It shows the result of picking the best option from four possibilities each quarter. Of course, the values shown require perfect timing — an unobtainable holy grail, but at least they show the scale of the potential value added. In fact, style timing can generate performance enhancement roughly of the same scale as traditional asset allocation.

Levis and Liodakis (1999) show the potential for gains from style rotation in the UK context. They consider an investor with a perfect foresight rotation strategy. That is she picks the best performing style (only two styles were included in their study). They found that between 1968 and 1997, such a gifted investor would have earned a 29.10% gross average annual return, or 24.51% net of 100 bp transaction costs per transaction. Against a benchmark of the FT-All Share returning 16%, this represents a potential gain of 19% gross!

The rest of this chapter deals with trying to find factors that drive the style rotation within markets, so that we can try and improve our timing ability to switch between value and growth.

3.5   LIFE CYCLE OF AN INVESTMENT STYLE

Before we explore the drivers behind style rotation, a short detour to an incredibly important paper is warranted. Barberis and Shleifer (2001) model a situation where an investor's behaviour is driven by relative (rather than absolute) returns. The model rests on two key assumptions. Firstly, money moves towards styles that have done relatively

Table 3.3 Potential gains from active management in the USA (1979–1994) (% p.a.)

Best possible asset allocation	31.93%
Static mix of equities, bonds and cash	13.2%
Possible gains	18.73%
Best possible style allocation	29.67%
Wiltshire 500	13.98%
Possible gains	15.69%

Source: First Madison Advisors.

well in the past (AKA preference for winners, positive feedback trading). A style could be any mental account that investors assign investments to. That is to say small cap/large cap, index trackers/active, value/growth or indeed stocks/bonds can all be viewed as an investment style within the discussion that follows.

Empirically, this certainly seems to be a reasonable assumption. Investors do seem to be attracted towards styles that have done well in the recent past. Sirri and Tufano (1998) study the flows of funds into 690 equity mutual funds in the period 1971–1990. They find that consumers appear to base their fund purchase decisions on prior performance information, but do so asymmetrically, investing in funds that performed very well the prior period. Sirri and Tufano's finding is supported by even more recent research by Odean (2001). As Figure 3.2 shows, money does indeed pour into mutual funds that tend to have done well in the recent past, with the top performing decile of mutual funds attracting a massive proportion of the inflows.

The second key assumption is that these flows of funds have an effect on the relative prices of these investments. Prices of favoured styles are driven up — possibly beyond the level warranted by the fundamentals — whilst those out of favour are driven down. The good performance of the successful style makes the competing style look bad in a relative sense. This in turn generates flows of funds from the relatively bad style to the relatively good style. In the technical jargon so beloved by economists this is known as a negative externality.

In order to generate these effects, the two are populated by two types of investors, fundamentalists and switchers. As the name suggests the fundamentalists are driven by the underlying fundamentals of each style. The switchers are akin to momentum traders (or positive feedback traders, if you prefer), and buy whichever style has recently outperformed (trend followers). This group essentially have adaptive expectations. Such expectations can be generated by the representativeness bias documented in Chapter 1. A style that has had several periods of high returns may be interpreted as representative of a style with a high true mean return. Alternatively adaptive expectations may be generated by agency considerations; actuaries may recommend

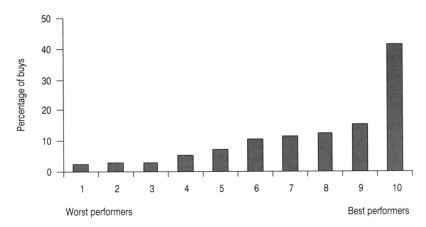

Figure 3.2   Flows into mutual funds — chasing returns
Source: Odean (2001).

fund managers be appointed on the basis of past performance purely because it is easy to justify ex post to the pension fund itself.

All of this may seem like the semantics of ivory tower-dwelling academics. However, the model actually generates patterns of behaviour very like those observed in financial markets. The model creates a life cycle for an investment style which will seem distinctly familiar to those who participate in the 'real' world of financial markets (Figure 3.3).

The birth of a style is engendered by good fundamentals about the style itself or bad fundamentals on the competing style (via the externality). The fundamental investors move their money on the basis of this driver. However, then the switchers start to observe the flows (or rather the price effects of the flows) of the fundamental investors. They then jump on the bandwagon. Slowly but surely, this new style gains attention, academics start to write papers investigating the style, and new funds are recruited to follow the style. Maturity occurs once the style is firmly embedded in the investor's psyche. Eventually, demise and rot set in, as either bad news on the fundamentals of the prevalent style is unearthed, or conversely, good news on the fundamentals of the competing style is uncovered.

3.5.1 Implications

This kind of model has several dramatic implications for real-world investors. Firstly, the true mean return for a style is virtually impossible to define. That is to say, we can never be sure if value or growth actually outperforms in the long run, because of the presence of the switchers. We only observe the total return from a particular style. It is impossible to decompose this into the component driven by the fundamental investors (the true mean) and the element attributable to the switchers.

This in turn has important implications for portfolio management. It suggests that styles that have performed extremely well in the past will be called into question when the tide turns against them even temporarily. Sounds distinctly familiar to anyone who has invested through the last decade or so.

Style investing may itself introduce co-movement of returns, even when the fundamentals are unrelated. These factors could generate higher average returns for

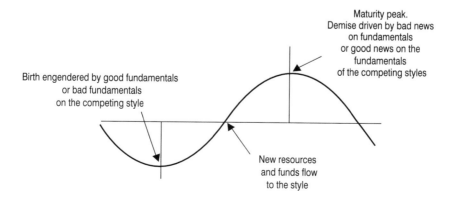

Figure 3.3   Life cycle of an investment style

reasons that are totally unrelated to risk, directly contrary to the efficient markets view that risk and return go hand in hand.

3.5.2   Examples: Return Co-movement

The twin security puzzle of Chapter 2 can be seen within this style investing framework. Take Royal Dutch Shell as an example. We showed in Chapter 2 that these two stocks are claims on the same cash flow, so in an efficient market they should trade in a constant ratio. However, Froot and Dabora (1999) show that Royal Dutch is more sensitive to moves in the US market, while Shell co-moves with the UK market. Royal Dutch is, of course, a member of the S&P500 and as such it gets buffeted by the flows of investors for whom the S&P500 is a style (i.e. index trackers and active managers with the S&P500 as a benchmark). Similarly, Shell is driven by its membership of the FTSE 100.

The shift within Europe to sector-based analysis away from country-based analysis can also be viewed within this context. The Barberis and Shleifer model would suggest that such a shift would lead to industry factors increasing in importance within returns, and country factors decreasing in importance in relative terms. Rouwenhorst (1999) documents that when this shift started country effects were still dominant. However, his more recent work shows that now industry risks are equally (if not more) important. This clearly shows that it was the shift in the allocation strategy that caused the change in the returns structure, rather than the other way around (Figure 3.4).

3.5.3   Examples: Style Life Cycles

The life cycle of value and growth stocks will take up most of the rest of this chapter. However, in order to demonstrate the power of Barberis and Shleifer's model we will examine a past potential example of a style life cycle — small cap investing. Small stock investing took off after Banz (1981) reported that small stocks tended to outperform

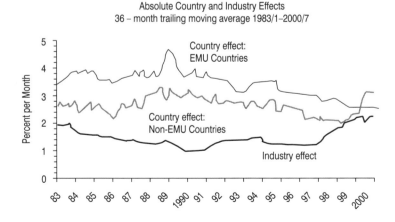

Figure 3.4   Relative importance of country vs. sector in EMU

Adapted from Rouwenhorst (1999), Financial Analysts Journal, with permission from the Association for Investment Management and Research.

large stocks on average. However, it should also be noted that small cap investing also took off after a period of dismal performance by the large caps. The Nifty Fifty (the large caps that were set to conquer the world) started to fail in 1973/4. Effectively each fell short of their expected earnings target and were taken out and shot one by one. The result was a flow of funds into small cap and a burst of small cap dominance in the period 1975–1983.

Of course, since then small caps have tended to underperform large caps. This large cap dominance has coincided with the rise of indexation, and increased focus on minimizing tracking errors amongst active fund managers generally. Gompers and Metrick (2001) show that institutional investors prefer large stocks and their ownership of such stocks has been rising rapidly in the last two decades. This increased demand for the competing style may be one reason for the relative underperformance of small stocks.

3.6.   VALUE VS. GROWTH: RISK OR BEHAVIOURAL?

Before turning to insights into timing style rotation, we need to assess whether the drivers of the value/growth relationship are behavioural- or risk-based. Much of this analysis will be covered in more depth in the next chapter on stock valuation.

The efficient market zealots would have us believe that only risk is priced in equilibrium, and hence the fact that value outperforms in the long run suggests to them that it must be a measure of risk. Fama and French (1993) hypothesize that the value premium is a return to a systemic dislike for financial distress. However, the value premium seems to be badly correlated with underlying factors of economic distress, such as number of defaults on corporate bonds or bankruptcy (Griffin and Lemmon, 2002).

In addition, Figure 3.5 shows the realized (ex post) annual standard deviations for the MSCI value and growth indices. It is clear that there is generally very little risk differential between the two. Of course, given the collapse of the internet bubble, growth stock volatility has rocketed (hence the spike in the latter part of the sample).

An alternative is that the value premium is the result of investors' behavioural biases. Could it be that investors simply become too pessimistic about value stocks during downturns, and too optimistic about growth stocks in upswings?

Chan, Karceski and Lakonishok (2000a) show that the recent dominance of large cap growth stocks appears to be unrelated to their fundamental performance. On a variety of measures they show that the operating performance of large cap growth stocks is nothing out of the ordinary, relative to their own past performance, and indeed relative to the operating performance of rival styles (Table 3.4).

In one crucial respect growth stocks are riskier than value stocks. Skinner and Sloan (1999) examine the behaviour of US value and growth stocks around earnings announcements in the period 1984–1996 (Figure 3.6). They find 'clear evidence of an asymmetrically large reaction to earnings disappointments for high growth firms'. For instance, a value stock that falls short of expectations by 5% tends to suffer a −6% abnormal return over the subsequent quarter. In contrast, a growth stock that misses expectations by the same margin of 5% suffers an average abnormal return in the region of −15% in the subsequent quarter. This should not come as a major surprise, after all if you have bought a growth stock you presumably expect it to deliver growth, and when it doesn't it gets severely punished.

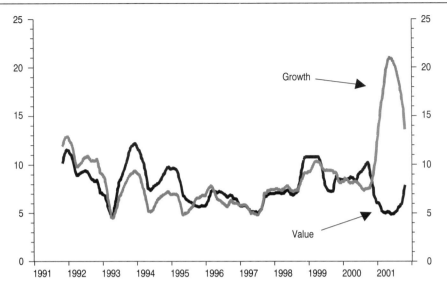

Figure 3.5 Value and growth — annual standard deviations of returns
Data Source: Thomson Datastream.

Table 3.4 US value vs. growth: the fundamentals

%	Small growth	Large growth	Small value	Large value
Sales growth				
1970–98	14.7	10.2	8.1	8.0
1970–79	15.2	14.3	10.9	13.4
1980–89	12.5	8.9	6.6	5.8
1990–98	16.5	7.5	6.8	4.8
Operating income before depreciation				
1970–98	13.8	10.6	12.5	7.1
1970–79	13.6	14.0	14.3	10.5
1980–89	11.1	8.4	11.2	5.1
1990–98	17.0	9.3	12.0	5.5
Dividend growth				
1970–98	12.3	10.9	11.2	6.0
1970–79	14.5	12.4	10.7	6.8
1980–89	13.0	9.7	14.4	7.0
1990–98	9.2	10.5	8.2	4.2

Adapted from Chan, Karceski and Lakonishok (2000a), Financial Analysts Journal, with permission from the Association for Investment Management and Research.

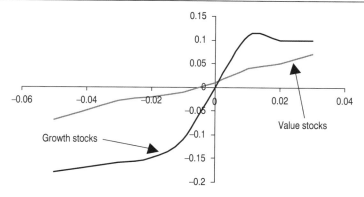

Figure 3.6 Earnings response functions
Source: Skinner and Sloan (1999).

Skinner and Sloan actually go further, 'after controlling for this effect, there is no evidence of a stock return differential between growth stocks and other stocks'. In other words, the long run outperformance of value stocks is actually driven by growth stocks falling short of expectations.

It may be the case that investors believe growth stocks will triumph in the future, and hence the late 1990s witnessed investors re-rating growth stocks on the basis of expected returns rather than past performance. However, it seems a leap of blind faith to place complete confidence in ephemeral future earnings with no foundation in recent history.

LaPorta (1996) provides some sobering findings for those who would make such a leap of faith. He focused on a large sample of US stocks. The universe was ranked on the basis of I/B/E/S consensus long-term earnings growth forecasts from analysts. LaPorta found that the stocks with the highest future returns earned much lower returns than those with the lowest growth forecast (Figure 3.7).

Chan, Karceski and Lakonishok (2000b) make a similar point. A cursory glance at Table 3.5 reveals that those stocks with the highest expected growth fail to deliver by the largest margin. Meanwhile the unloved value stocks (low expected growth) manage to exceed the overly pessimistic forecasts offered up by analysts.

Chan, Karceski and Lakonishok do not stop there. They go on to show that very few firms experience persistence in their operating performance. They examine the number of firms that deliver above median growth in three income statement lines — sales, operating income before depreciation, and income before extraordinaries. The resulting percentages are compared with those that would be expected randomly (i.e. 50% of firms should be above the median in the first year, and so forth).

Interestingly, the higher up the income statement you move, the more persistence you encounter. This in itself could suggest that managers focus too much on keeping sales steady (high), at the expense of profitability. It should also be noted that it suggests price to sales is a highly dubious valuation metric!

Table 3.6 shows the results of Chan, Karceski and Lakonishok's work on income before extraordinaries for a number of styles/sectors. By and large persistence seems to be extremely elusive. So investors building their hopes on growth stocks generating long

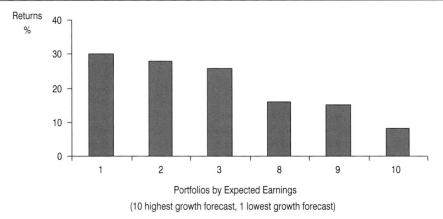

Figure 3.7 High growth = huge disappointment

Source: LaPorta (1996). Reproduced from Blackwell Publishers.

Table 3.5 Realized vs. forecast earnings growth

	1 (Low expected growth)	2	3	4	5 (High expected growth)
Median IBES long-term earnings growth forecast	5.9	10.2	12.3	15.0	22.4
1 Year realized growth	11.4	13.1	13.0	14.1	19.1
3 Year realized growth	9.7	11.2	10.4	11.5	12.5
5 Year realized growth	8.8	10.5	10.0	10.8	11.1

Source: Chan, Karceski and Lakonishok (2000b).

Table 3.6 Persistence of growth in income before extraordinaries (% of firms with above median growth each year for the number of years)

Years/sector	1	2	3	4	5	6	7	8	9	10
Tech stocks	50.9	25.9	13.5	7.3	4.1	2.5	1.5	0.9	0.5	0.4
Value	48.3	23.8	11.4	5.4	2.5	1.2	0.7	0.4	0.3	0.2
Growth	50.7	25.2	12.0	5.8	2.9	1.6	0.9	0.4	0.2	0.1
Large cap	46.7	21.9	10.0	4.7	2.2	1.2	0.7	0.4	0.3	0.2
Mid-cap	49.4	24.9	12.4	6.2	3.1	1.6	0.9	0.5	0.3	0.2
Small cap	51.0	25.5	12.6	6.3	3.2	1.7	0.9	0.4	0.2	0.1
Expected	50.0	25.0	12.5	6.3	3.1	1.6	0.8	0.4	0.2	0.1

Source: Chan, Karceski and Lakonishok (2000b).

run superior operating performance should think twice ... such assumptions rest on very shaky foundations.

The aim of this section has been to demonstrate that there are a number of very good reasons to believe the market's pricing of value and growth stocks is not driven purely by risk factors, but rather that sentiment and psychology play a large (dominant) role. This theme will be investigated further in the next chapter (on stock valuation), where more rigorous evidence of the behavioural basis for value and growth performance will be given. However, providing the reader is sufficiently convinced that this is the case, we can move onwards towards a discussion of style rotation.

3.7 STYLE ROTATION

Behavioural finance is sometimes accused of schizophrenia for predicting momentum returns on the one hand and contrarian effects on the other. For instance, Jegadeesh and Titman (1993, 1999) show that over a 3–12 month period, past winners (past positive price or earnings momentum) outperform past losers. However, DeBondt and Thaler (1985) and Lakonishok, Shleifer and Vishny (1994) show that over long horizons (3–5 years) long-term winners (high returns over the past five years, high price to book ratio or high sales/earnings growth) underperform long-term losers (low returns over the past five years, low price to book ratios or low sales/earnings growth).

A spurt of recent research amongst behavioural finance academics has led to a number of models that seek to marry these two effects — short-term momentum and longer-term reversals — in a common framework. These include three particularly notable studies. Firstly, Barberis, Shleifer and Vishny (1998) rely on conservatism (anchoring) and representativeness biases to generate initial under-reaction and subsequent over-reaction. Hong and Stein (1999) rely on a form of bounded rationality of two kinds of investors, news watchers and momentum traders (the parallels with the Barberis and Shleifer life cycle model are obvious, except that Hong and Stein don't model an externality, and their results aren't based on relative performance). Finally, Daniel, Hirschleifer and Subrahmanyam (1999a) rely on over-confidence and self-attribution biases to generate momentum reversals. In their model, investors first estimate the value of an investment, and then estimate the precision of their valuation. Because of self-attribution bias, investors overweight information that confirms their original view, and underweight information that is inconsistent with their original view. As a result, their estimate of the precision of their valuation increases over time, leading to momentum as a sort of delayed over-reaction if you like.

Experimentalists have recently turned their attention to studying the behaviour that could cause both under- and over-reaction. Bloomfield, Libby and Nelson (2000a) report two experiments that examine whether people tend to overweight old elements of earnings time series in a manner that produces predictable under- and over-reactions to current earnings changes and levels. In the first experiment, MBA students used annual returns on equity (ROE) information to predict future annual ROE, which determines the value of securities they traded in a laboratory market. In the second experiment, experienced financial analysts used quarterly earnings information to predict future quarterly earnings. In both experiments, participants relied too heavily on older time series information. This single misweighting error caused apparent under-reaction to earnings changes or over-reactions to sustained earnings levels, depending on the particular time series observed. This study lends support to the Barberis, Shleifer and Vishny model of style rotation.

In Bloomfield and Hales (2001) two experiments with MBA student participants support Barberis, Shleifer and Vishny's (1998) prediction that investors expect random walk sequences to shift between continuation regimes (in which changes tend to be followed by like changes) and reversal regimes (in which changes tend to be followed by reverse changes). As predicted, investors over-reacted to changes that were preceded by many continuations, and under-reacted to changes that were preceded by many reversals.

Bloomfield, Libby and Nelson (2000b) show that when investors receive only a noisy signal of the reliability of their information, they will tend to under-react to reliable information (such as recent earnings announcements) but over-react to unreliable information (such as analysts' long-term growth forecasts). This finding is supported by the work of Griffin and Tversky (1992). Daniel and Titman (2000) suggest that over-confidence is likely to be at its highest where there is a low visibility of underlying data. Hence private information will not be challenged in such a strong way. This suggests that over-confidence mispricing effects are more likely to be seen in growth stocks.

Interestingly, the three models outlined above give generally similar predictions about the nature of style rotation. However, at the time of writing the Barberis, Shleifer and Vishny model seems to have the slight edge in terms of empirical support. Swaminathan and Lee (2000) present a graphical representation (Figure 3.8) of these behavioural models, which they call the momentum life cycle.

According to the momentum life cycle hypothesis, stocks are subject to bouts of under-reaction and over-reaction, and investors' favouritism and neglect. A stock with positive momentum (either in terms of earnings or price) would be on the left-hand side of the diagram. These stocks are past winners. Stocks with negative momentum (either in terms of price or earnings) would be on the right-hand side of the diagram. These stocks are past losers.

Stocks which experience good news move up the cycle, eventually becoming the stock of the moment, or a glamour stock if you prefer. Eventually, these stocks disappoint the market and experience big negative surprises. Stocks that then continue to disappoint begin an inexorable decline, and end up suffering general neglect. At this point they tend to become value stocks, attracting the attention of contrarian investors.

The lower left quadrant and upper right quadrant are characterized by investor under-reaction. Early stage winners have experienced a long period of declining earnings and stock prices, but have recently experienced positive surprises and a bounce in stock prices. Early stage losers have the opposite pattern — a history of good earnings and positive share price momentum, but then they suffer a negative surprise and the stock price starts to decline. In both cases, investors tend to under-react assuming (over-optimistically and over-confidently) that their forecasts are correct and that current conditions are nothing but a blip. The truth of the matter is very different.

The upper left and lower right quadrants are characterized by investor over-reaction. Late stage winners have a long history of good performance with solid earnings growth. However, investors simply become too enamoured with these stocks — expecting them to be invincible. Hence expectations are ratcheted up and up, until such time as the

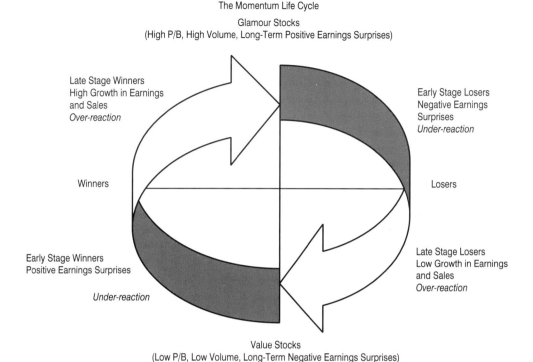

Figure 3.8   The momentum life cycle

Source: Swaminathan and Lee (2000).

stock delivers a negative surprise. Late stage losers tend to have a long track record of poor earnings performance and disappointing share price returns. Here investors become overly pessimistic about the ability of these stocks to ever recover. Thus both late stage winners and losers witness investors extrapolating present trends too far into the future.

Given the presence of under-reaction in the early stage winners and losers, and over-reaction in the late stage winners and losers, it should be expected that early stage winners outperform late stage winners and that early stage losers underperform late stage losers. Swaminathan and Lee present careful data analysis that confirms that these predictions are recorded in the US market. Further supporting evidence is found in Daniel and Titman (2000). They essentially test that early stage winners outperform late stage winners (Figure 3.9). They find that high momentum, low price to book stocks significantly outperform low momentum, high price to book stocks. A zero net investment portfolio on this basis did extremely well, generating profits in 31 out of 34 years, with an annual average profit of 12.5%, a CAPM beta of −0.258 and a Sharpe ratio of 1.12.

The key message to take away from all of this analysis is that early stage winners and losers exhibit return continuation — momentum trading works in these quadrants.

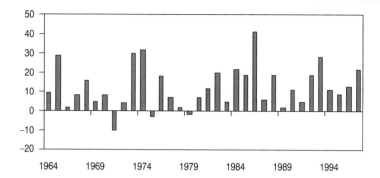

Figure 3.9   Long early stage winners, short late stage winners
Reproduced from Daniel and Titman (1999), Financial Analysts Journal, with
permission from the Association for Investment Management and Research.

Late stage winners and losers tend to exhibit return reversals — contrarian strategies
work in these quadrants. Given that we know the time horizons involved in each style
(momentum 3–12 months, contrarian 3–5 years) we can start to construct rotational
models that should generate significant alpha.

3.8   QUANTITATIVE SCREENS

Perhaps the single most obvious way of timing the switch between styles is to use some
form of quantitative screen. The momentum life cycle hypothesis clearly tells us what
we should be looking for. Amongst value stocks (low price to book, low volume, long
history of earnings disappointments) we should be searching for stocks that have just
started to deliver good news. Amongst glamour stocks (high price to book, high
volume, long history of exceeding earnings expectations) we should be hunting out
those stocks that have just started to deliver disappointing results.

One of the great advantages of a quantitative screen is that it is done by computers.
This removes the psychological bias from the process. The screen doesn't care whether
the stock is a dog or not, it concerns itself only with whether the stock fits the criteria
built into its program. Some fund managers such as ABN Amro are now using exactly
this sort of screen in a fund explicitly designed to exploit the theories of behavioural
finance.

3.8.1   Value Strategies

Piotroski (2000) presents an interesting premise. He asks if the use of simple
accounting-based analysis can improve value stock selection. He finds that less than
44% of all low market to book firms earn positive excess returns in the two years
following portfolio formation. He shows that using a simple accounting screen
improves the mean return to a low price to book investor by at least 7.5% annually.
The entire distribution of returns is shifted to the right. He suggests using a very simple
binary classification system based on the following indicators.

3.8.1.1 Profitability

Current profitability and cash flow realizations provide information about a firm's ability to generate funds internally. Given poor historical earnings performance of value firms, any firm currently generating positive cash flows or profits is demonstrating a capacity to generate some funds through operating activity. A positive earnings trend is suggestive of an improvement in the firm's underlying ability to generate positive cash flows.

- ROA
  Net income before extraordinary items/total assets
  >0, then 1 else 0
- CFO
  Cash flow from operations/total assets
  >0, then 1 else 0
- ΔROA
  >0, then 1 else 0
- Accruals
  CFO > ROA, then 1 else 0

3.8.1.2 Leverage, Liquidity and Source of Funds

These indicators are designed to measure changes in capital structure and the firm's ability to meet future debt service obligations. Since most low price to book firms are financially constrained, an increase in leverage, deterioration of liquidity or the use of external financing is a bad signal about financial risk.

- ΔLever
  Changes in the firm's long-term debt levels. Measured as the historical change in the ratio of long-term debt to average total assets. If leverage fell 1, else 0.
- ΔLiquid
  Historical change in the firm's current ratio between the current and prior year, where the current ratio is defined as the ratio of current assets to current liabilities. If liquidity > 0 then 1, else 0.
- Equity offering
  1 if the firm didn't issue equity in the preceding 12 months.

3.8.1.3 Operating Efficiency

- ΔMargin
  Defined as the firm's current gross margin ratio (gross margin scaled by total sales) less the prior year's gross margin ratio. An improvement in margins signifies a potential improvement in factor costs, a reduction in inventory costs or a price increase. If >0 then 1 else 0.
- ΔTurnover
  Defined as firm's current year asset turnover ratio (total sales scaled by assets) less the prior year's asset turnover. An improvement in asset turnover signifies greater productivity from the asset base.

A composite score is then created by summing across the various categories. Piotroski examined the US market between 1976 and 1996. He formed market to book quintiles. Firms in the lowest market to book quintile are used as value stocks. This yields a final sample of 14,043 firms across the 12 years. Returns are measured as one year buy and hold.

Piotroski then formed two portfolios, low score (those with 0 or 1 score) and high score (8 or 9). For the complete low price to book portfolio consistent with the extant literature, a 6% value premium is found. However, it is highly concentrated. Only 43% of firms generate a positive excess return over the year following formation. Sorting on score revealed that financially strong firms outperformed. This is of course in direct violation of the efficient markets view that the higher return on low price to book stocks is the result of a risk proxy for financial distress (Table 3.7).

Figure 3.10 shows the annual returns to buying scores ⩾5, and shorting scores <5. Such a strategy yields an annual average return of 9%, and a Sharpe ratio of 1.10. It suggests that investors can do well from using a quantitative financial health screen when dealing with value stocks.

Table 3.7   Returns by financial soundness

Score	Mean excess return	NOBS
0	−6	57
1	−10	339
2	−2	859
3	−1.5	1618
4	2.6	2462
5	5.2	2787
6	11.2	2579
7	11.6	1894
8	12.7	1115
9	15.8	333

Source: Piotroski (2000).

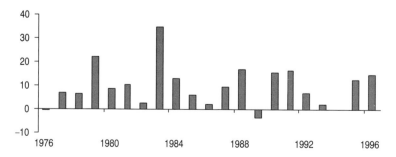

Figure 3.10   Long financial soundness, short financial vulnerability

Reproduced from Piotroski, 'Value Investing', Journal of Accounting Research, Vol 38 (2000), with permission from Blackwell Publishers.

3.9   TIMING THE SWITCH

3.9.1   The Equity Risk Premium

One of the measures that we have found to be successful at timing investors' style rotation has been the implied equity risk premium. If the rotation between value and growth is driven by an investor's subjective beliefs, then we need to find proxy measures for the fear and greed inherent in the equity markets. We construct a very simple measure of the implied equity risk premium.

Here we define the implied equity risk premium as follows:

$$\text{Implied ERP} = (100/12 \text{ month forward consensus PE}) - \text{Long-term growth}$$

$$- \text{ Current 10 year bond yield}$$

We generally use the long-run economic growth rate as the proxy for long-term growth, as it is impossible for dividend/earnings growth to exceed economic growth in the very long run. Figure 3.11 shows the relationship between value/growth and the implicit ERP for the US market. It certainly seems to capture the turning points relatively well.

The reason that the ERP seems to work lies in the fact that the ERP can be seen as a proxy for investors' time horizons. As we showed in Chapter 1, Benartzi and Thaler (1995) have combined prospect theory and myopia to discuss the ERP. They produced the chart in Figure 3.12 showing the linkage between time horizon and ERP.

Value and growth also have an interpretation in the time domain. As DeChow, Sloan and Soliman (2001) show, price to book serves as a noisy proxy for implied equity duration. Duration is a concept more usually associated with bonds than equities. However, it can be useful to think in terms of equity duration. Essentially, duration refers to the change in an instrument's return for a one percentage point interest rate move. The measure captures not only how much return an investor might expect, but also when to expect it. Duration can be thought of as a weighted average maturity, and hence it is measured in years. For example, consider two 30 year bonds — similar in

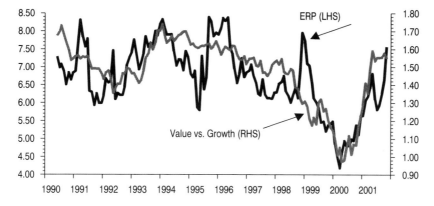

Figure 3.11   Implied equity risk premium and value vs. growth
Data Source: Thomson Datastream.

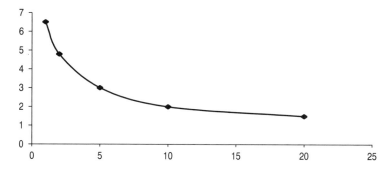

Figure 3.12 Time horizons and equity risk premium

Source: Reproduced from Benartzi and Thaler, The Quarterly Journal of Economics, 110:1 (Feb 1995), pp. 73–92, Copyright 1995, with permission from MIT Press.

every respect except that one is a standard coupon paying note, the other is a zero coupon bond. The 30 year coupon paying note will reward its owner each and every year, whilst the zero coupon bond only pays out in the 30th year. The coupon bearing bond will thus have a shorter weighted average maturity or lower duration than the zero coupon bond.

Within the equity arena, duration can be thought of as a measure of the certainty of return that investors anticipate. Total stock returns can, of course, be split into two elements — dividend yield and capital appreciation. Dividend yield is the more predictable of the two components. Investors know when and (if the analysts are accurate, a big if for sure) roughly how much to expect from each dividend payout. The capital appreciation element is much more uncertain. Markets or stocks with higher dividend yield have a more certain return, and hence a lower duration. Of course, value stocks tend to have much higher dividend yields than growth stocks, hence they are shorter duration assets.

If the implied ERP drops then it is equivalent to saying that investors have extended their time horizon. Given that growth stocks, by their very nature, are longer duration assets, an increasing time horizon means that investors will favour such stocks. Conversely, when certainty of return is foremost in people's minds, the implied ERP ratchets up, investors shrink their time horizons, and it is value stocks that should benefit.

3.9.2 The Payout Ratio

The dividend payout ratio also seems to act as a reasonable timing signal for value/growth rotation. In general, we have observed that value seems to outperform during the economic good times, and growth during the economic bad times. This was clearly not the case during the internet bubble period of the very late 1990s, once again confirming the bubble nature of the period.

However in more normal times, the dividend payout ratio seems to signal turning points in the value/growth cycle well. Dividend signalling has received much attention in the academic literature, ever since Lintner (1956) found that firms tend to smooth dividends so as not to disappoint investors. Figure 3.13 shows the relationship between the payout ratio and value vs. growth. Most of the time, value outperforms after the

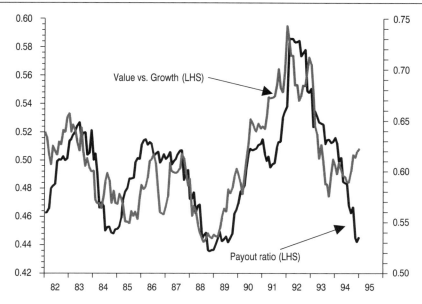

Figure 3.13 Payout ratio and value vs. growth
Data Source: Thomson Datastream.

dividend payout ratio has bottomed, while growth outperforms when the payout ratio troughs.

Bernstein (1995) points out that because dividends are less volatile than earnings, monitoring the dividend payout ratio is a way of tracking 'permanent' or 'normalized' earnings. In other words, if the payout ratio is towards the bottom of its long run range, then earnings have been quite strong recently, and the odds are that earnings will weaken in the future. Conversely, if the dividend payout ratio is high then earnings have been relatively weak, and the odds favour an improvement in the economy and the earnings outlook.

3.9.3 IPOs

A second potential timing device is to use data on new equity issuance. It is well documented that IPOs move in cycles, both in terms of initial return and volume. We will explore why this is so in Chapter 7 on corporate finance. However, Figures 3.14 and 3.15 illustrate the cyclical nature of the IPO market for the US.

Think about the style characteristics of IPOs. Firms coming to the market tend to be small cap growth stocks. So when the window for IPOs is at its widest, it is small cap growth that is likely to be leading the market. The small cap growth sector, once it is out of favour for more than a month or two, tends to stay out of favour for several years. Currently, it has been out of favour for about a year.

Though the 1974–1981 period is the most extreme example of this sector's unpopularity, there are others. Small growth stocks also remained out of favour for

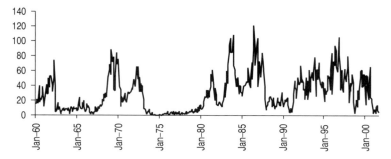

Figure 3.14 IPOs per month — volume
Source: Ritter (1998).

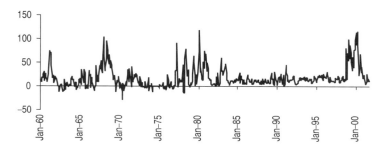

Figure 3.15 IPO initial returns
Source: Ritter (1998).

about five years in the early 1960s, during which IPO volume nearly dried up. These stocks also succumbed to the crash of 1987, and on that occasion as well, low IPO activity persisted for several more years. Keeping an eye on the volume of IPOs passing through the market would seem to be a good indicator of which style is prevalent, and as we will show in Chapter 6 IPO data can be used to time the market more broadly than just style rotation.

3.10 CONCLUSIONS

The most important conclusion of this chapter is that we simply don't know whether value or growth outperforms in the long run. The evidence that any differential between value and growth stocks has a psychological basis seems overwhelming to us.

In order to exploit these behavioural errors, and to avoid the potential disaster of getting anchored to one style, rotation appears to be the optimal approach. What is more, style rotation offers potential gains of the same order of magnitude as traditional asset allocation. Yet only a fraction of the resources offered to asset allocation are devoted to style rotation.

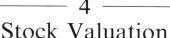

4
Stock Valuation

It is not a case of choosing those which, to the best of one's judgement, are the prettiest, nor even those which average opinion genuinely thinks the prettiest. We have reached the third degree, where we devote our intelligence to anticipating what average opinion expects the average opinion to be. And there are some, I believe, who practice the fourth, fifth and higher degrees.

John Maynard Keynes

4.1 INTRODUCTION

How should we value a company? This is one of the most important questions facing analysts and investors alike. It lies at the very heart of the investment decision. Yet the structures of classical finance are still used blithely, indeed so deeply ingrained are the assumptions so common to classical finance, most analysts and investors don't even realize they are implicitly assuming such nonsensical things as market efficiency. In this chapter we will expand on several issues already raised in Chapter 1 — on anchoring and framing — and in addition we will examine the best way in which to incorporate behavioural insights into your valuation methodology. But first let's return to Keynes' beauty contest.

4.2 KEYNES' BEAUTY COMPETITION

John Maynard Keynes was not only an outstanding economist, but also a canny investor who not only made several fortunes on the stock exchange but also lost several as well. Indeed, the quotation from the general theory that starts this chapter shows roughly what Keynes thought of the market.

The immediate relevancy of the quotation from Keynes will strike anyone who has spent the last few years pondering the market's treatment of internet stocks. A great many institutional investors knew the valuations attached to internet stocks were insane, yet there was a vast performance loss associated with actually implementing this view, as the prices of these stocks were pushed even higher. The result was a situation we described in Chapter 2 — positive feedback — the optimal strategy was to buy these stocks even if you didn't believe the market, if you thought you could sell them at a higher price to other investors.

A simple game captures both this reasoning and that behind Keynes' view. In a typical beauty contest game, participants are asked to simultaneously pick a number between 0 and 100, and told that two thirds of the average number picked will be the winning number. The player who is closest to this target (two thirds of the average) wins a predefined prize.

The beauty contest can be used to assess whether people are really practicing 'fourth, fifth, or higher degrees' as Keynes hypothesized. Here is a typical thought process when faced with this game. Assume the average is 50, then you should choose 33, to be closest to the target of two thirds of the average and hence win. But if you think that all the other players will choose this, then to be one step ahead of the game you need to pick two thirds of 33 (22). Of course, if you have thought of that so may they, hence you need to be two steps ahead and pick 15 (rounded to the nearest whole number). And so forth.

In fact, the stable equilibrium is zero — game theorists call this a Nash equilibrium. The beauty contest is a neat measure of the number of steps of thinking that the players are doing. The beauty contest has been played out with a very large number of subject groups, including corporate CEOs, economics PhDs, game theorists and readers of the financial press (the *FT* in the UK, *Spektrum* in Germany and *Expansion* in Spain). The results show a remarkable consistency (Figures 4.1–4.3). Players use 0–3 levels of reasoning, and very few players pick the Nash equilibrium of zero (see Nagel, 1999 for a survey of these examples[1]).

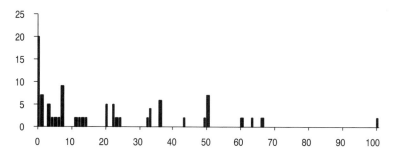

Figure 4.1 The game theorists' view

Source: Adapted from Nagel (1999). Reproduced with permission from Lawrence Erlbaum Associates.

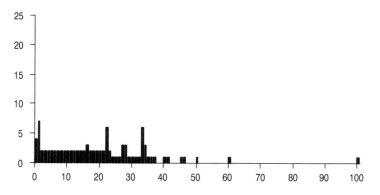

Figure 4.2 The newspaper players

Source: Adapted from Nagel (1999). Reproduced with permission from Lawrence Erlbaum Associates.

---

[1] For those interested in behavioural game theory, Colin Camerer is in the process of writing an excellent book on the subject. He includes a whole chapter on games like the beauty contest. Camerer (forthcoming), *Behavioural Game Theory: Experiments on Strategic Interaction*.

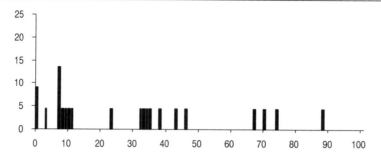

Figure 4.3   A leading fund management group
Source: DKWR.

The fact that most players seem to use 0–3 levels of reasoning fits well with the idea of persistent bubbles in stock markets. Even if all investors think there is a crash coming they don't iterate their thinking back to the present. They guess that others will sell a couple of steps before the crash, and plan to sell just before that exodus.

4.3   THE (IR)RELEVANCE OF FUNDAMENTALS

Determining fundamental value lies at the heart of much of the work done in financial markets. Analysts spend hours and hours poring over spreadsheets, modelling the minutiae of firms' financial details — desperately trying to divine the Holy Grail of 'fair value'.

To some extent these efforts are misplaced. Evidence from experimental markets shows that deviations from fundamental value can persist for very long periods. Because the experimental markets are, of course, artificial it is possible to control the information flow in a way we are unable to do in real-world financial markets.

Caginalp, Porter and Smith (2000) provide a great overview of the results from this area. According to them 'In a typical laboratory experiment, a group of subjects participate in a trading session lasting approximately two hours. Each subject is given a certain amount of stock and cash with which to trade. Trading is conducted via computers over a local area network, and the session is divided into fifteen periods. In each period, bids and offers are matched and trades clear simultaneously'.

Caginalp, Porter and Smith report several experiments where at the beginning of the session the participants are told that the stock may pay a dividend. The payoff is uncertain, but the distribution is known. Table 4.1 shows the distribution as it was given to the subjects. Participants were also told that the stock would be worthless at the end of the experiment, and they were told there were no shut-down costs.

If one follows the edicts of classical finance, and the dividend discount model, it is trivial to work out that the expected dividend is 24 cents, and thus the fair value of the stock in the first period is 324 (24×15) cents, decreasing by 24 cents per period. That at least is the theory in this full information market.

However, the reality was found to be frighteningly different. Figure 4.4 shows the market prices uncovered when three sets of subjects were put to the test. The three

Table 4.1   Dividend distribution

Probability	Payoff (in cents)
0.25	0
0.25	8
0.25	28
0.25	60

Source: Caginalp *et al.* (2000). Reproduced with permission from Lawrence Erlbaum Associates.

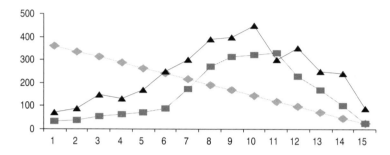

Figure 4.4   Bubbles in experimental markets
Source: Caginalp *et al.* (2000). Reproduced with permission from Lawrence Erlbaum Associates.

groups were economics undergraduates, economics postgraduates and a group of business executives.

The unconnected dashes in the chart represent fundamental value as determined by applying the dividend discount model. This was also the price at which the market consisting of postgraduate economists traded. So if the world were populated by trained economists (a scary thought I know) and information were full then the market might perhaps be said to be efficient.

However, thankfully for just about everyone the world isn't populated entirely by economists. The world would almost certainly be a very dull place, and most people reading this would be out of a job (incidentally, so would the author!).

The other two groups produced a very different picture. The undergraduate economics students managed to produce a serious price bubble — starting with a price that was less than 10% of fundamental value, and a peak in the discrepancy between price and value of 270%.

The business executives did even worse. They started slightly better with an initial price that was 20% of fundamental value. However, the peak discrepancy between price and value was a staggering 530%. Bear in mind that these are the simplest possible markets where information is fully and freely available, and there isn't much doubt as to future value. Despite these 'ideal' conditions, speculative bubbles still arose.

Caginalp, Porter and Smith point out that booms tend to be of long duration (10–11 periods) and also note the massive volume of trades (five to six times the outstanding stock of shares over the 15 period experiments). In general, the experimental evidence has shown that speculative bubbles are more likely to emerge where:

- The ratio of inexperienced to experienced traders is high.
- The uncertainty over fundamental value is greater.
- The lottery characteristics of the security are higher (though the chance is small, a very significant payoff is possible).
- Buying on margin is possible.
- Short selling is difficult.

So both the example of a beauty contest, and the overwhelming evidence from experimental markets, suggest bubbles in stock prices are all too possible. However, that is unlikely to stop the endeavours of Wall Street's army of analysts from combing through endless reams of corporate reports in order to generate some notion of fundamental value. It is to this process that we now turn.

4.4   VALUATION AND BEHAVIOURAL BIASES

We have already outlined in Chapter 1 the two main behavioural biases as they apply to the valuation process, but based on the number of times I have seen such errors be made by senior and experienced analysts, they certainly bear repeating.

Analysts are plagued by both agency problems and behavioural biases that lead them to be overly optimistic. Analysts face incentives to ingratiate themselves with the management of the companies they cover in order to gain access to information, to benefit the corporate finance side of the investment bank, to enhance the stocks held in-house by brokerage departments, and perhaps even to support the prices of stocks they hold themselves.

However, these agency issues are likely to be reinforced by natural optimism as outlined in Chapter 1. That is the illusion of control and related arguments suggest that analysts will 'feel' close to the companies they cover, and hence tend to be overly optimistic about their prospects.

Table 4.2 shows the distributions of analysts' recommendations as at the end of December 2001. The sheer scale of the recommendation imbalances is breathtaking. The tiny amount of negative recommendations once again suggests massive optimism in general.

The other area that attracts vast amounts of attention is the degree of bias within analysts' earnings forecasts. Figure 4.5 shows the average forecast error [defined as (forecast level – actual level)/actual level] between 1986 and 2000. The walk down to

Table 4.2   The distribution of analysts' recommendations (%)

	Buy	Hold	Sell
US	62	35	3
Japan	34	56	10
UK	48	37	15
Germany	47	36	17

Source: Bloomberg.

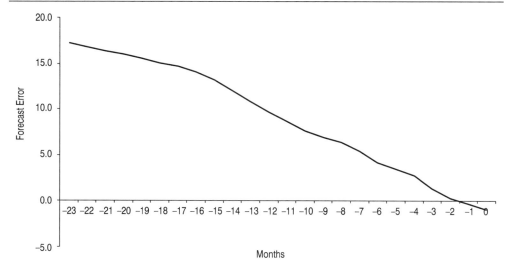

Figure 4.5   The walk down to beatable earnings: average forecast error (earnings level %)
Source: DKWR.

beatable earnings forecasts becomes immediately transparent. Analysts start forecasting 24 months ahead with initial forecasts on average some 17% higher than the actual outcome. By the time of the actual earnings announcement, analysts' expectations are just below the actual outcome.

4.4.1   Absolute Not Relative Valuation

As valuation textbooks like Cornell (1993) make clear, the only truly valid valuation measure is discounted cash flow (DCF). All relative valuation measures should be ignored. It is simply far too easy for an analyst to fixate (anchor, see Chapter 1) on her sector average as the 'correct' value. For instance, I have in the past been asked by analysts to construct tables of valuations on criteria such as price/earnings multiples or price/book multiples across industries, so that the analyst can then compare the stock under investigation with its peer group. This tells us nothing about the true 'fair value' of the equity.

However, this doesn't stop analysts using such methods in determining the attractiveness of shares. Bradshaw (2000) investigates the way in which analysts use their earnings forecasts in reaching their stock recommendations. Bradshaw notes that sell-side analysts summarize their opinions about a stock with earnings forecasts and stock recommendations. Because earnings forecasts reflect future fundamentals, and future fundamentals should determine value, forecasts and recommendations should be related. Using analysts' forecasts for earnings and a residual income valuation framework, Bradshaw finds that analysts' stock recommendations are unrelated to deviations from the intrinsic value. This confirms Block's (1999) conclusion that present value 'techniques are not used as widely in practice as they are in theory'.

Bradshaw tests an alternative hypothesis that analysts set their stock recommendations via the use of an earnings heuristic, especially the PE/G ratio (the ratio of the price earnings ratio to the forecast long-term growth rate). Depressingly, Bradshaw reports that stock recommendations and PE/G are closely correlated, that is to say despite all the emphasis in the literature on present value techniques, simply PE/G ratios are 'more' important in determining the stock recommendation that an analyst is likely to issue.

Even DCF has been diminished as a tool for valuation, because analysts are effectively anchored on the market price. Instead of building the valuation model from the bottom up, analysts tend to anchor on the current market price, trying to keep their valuation estimates close to it. Brav and Lehavy (2001) examine the relationship and dynamics between analysts' target prices and actual market prices. In line with previous studies (such as Womack, 1996) they show that analysts have short-run investment value — that is to say the spread in the average announcement day abnormal returns between positive and negative target price revisions is as high as 7%.

However, they also investigate the long-term dynamics of the relationship between target prices and actual prices. In 'equilibrium' they find that a typical firm's one year ahead target price is 22% higher than the current market price. The half-life of disturbances to this equilibrium is around 10 weeks. Most interestingly of all, they show that adjustments towards this long-term equilibrium are made virtually totally by revisions to the analyst's target price!

That is to say if a stock price drops, then in theory if the analyst were correct in their initial price target, it should become an even more attractive buy. However, in practice, analysts actually reduce their target prices in response to a drop in the current market price. For an in-depth case study of the pro-cyclicity of analysts' recommendations and stock prices see Cornell (2000) who investigates the case of Intel on Thursday 21 September 2000. On that day, Intel dropped some 30% in reaction to a press announcement, which stated, among other things, that the company expected revenue for the third quarter to be 3–5% higher than second quarter revenue of $8.3 billion. This fell short of the company's previous forecast of 7–9% growth and fell short of analysts' projections of 8–12%.

The market's response was astonishing. Although trading in Intel was halted for the remainder of the day after the announcement at 4:16, the stock dropped in after-market trading from the 'close' of $61.48 to $48.25 — erasing over $91 billion in market value. Over the next two days, the price continued to fall. By the close on September 26 2000, the stock was down almost 30% to $43.31, and $122 billion in shareholder value had evaporated.

Cornell (2000) builds a DCF model for Intel, and shows that even incorporating the news in the press announcement about the new level of revenue, the market was displaying a massive over-reaction. Yet despite this, analysts were far happier recommending the stock when it was at $76, than when it was at $40 per share! Little wonder that sell-side analysts have such dubious reputations.

As noted earlier, reverse engineered models are becoming more standard. These models attempt to back out growth rates for cash flows from the current market price. These can then be compared to the analysts' bottom-up model to assess the probability of achieving them. Buy-side analysts and fund managers are increasingly turning to such models, however, the sell side has been slower in adopting this approach.

4.4.2   Cash Flows Not Earnings

The second vital behavioural bias that must be remembered in the valuation process is narrow framing. Remember this is where we fail to see through the way in which information is actually presented (see Chapter 1, p. 12). We have already noted that it should be cash flows rather than earnings that analysts focus on (see Chapter 1, p. 13). However, few analysts bother to drill down into cash flow analysis, preferring instead to offer up opinions on earnings reported on some arbitrary accounting definition. Indeed in his study of industries' standard practices, Block (1999) found that a majority of analysts ranked earnings as a more important tool than cash flows (Table 4.3).

Further evidence of narrow framing amongst analysts is demonstrated by Teoh, Welch and Wong (1998a,b) in the context of initial public offerings, and seasoned equity offerings. They show that analysts fail to incorporate information about a firm's level of accruals into their forecasts. In fact, they show that analysts tend to have higher forecasts with stocks for higher accruals, in direct contrast to the observed reality that high accruals tend to underperform. Chan *et al.* (2001) show that high accrual firms exhibit high levels of past earnings and sales growth. If analysts are extrapolating past income statement performance, then they are suffering bias generated by the representativeness heuristic.

As we noted in Chapter 1 (p. 12), it is clear that a profit can be made by exploiting an earnings quality trade focusing on going long firms with low accruals, and short firms with high accruals. Yet, analysts ignore this information when forming their forecasts. Indeed, Richardson (2000) shows that the accruals trade is an unexploited opportunity. He finds that short sellers tend to concentrate on 'glamour' (high price to book) stocks, and don't seem to take advantage of the earnings quality trade.

It has long been known that it is possible to decompose returns into those generated by expectations about cash flow, and expectations on discount rates (expected returns) (see Campbell and Shiller, 1988). However, until recently only market-level returns have been examined. The conclusions from these studies show that it is clearly expected returns (or changes in the discount rate) that account for the vast majority of market-level return variance. However, recently Vuolteenaho (2001) has extended this framework to firm-level data. He shows that at the individual stock level expectations about cash flows are about twice as important as changes in the discount rate in explaining the variance of stock-level returns. That is firm-level stock returns are predominantly driven by expectations about cash flows. Analysts need to put cash flows at the heart of their analysis if they are to gain further insight into equity valuation.

Table 4.3   Rank of inputs in importance

Variable	First	Second	Third
Earnings	156	118	23
Cash flow	133	140	19
Book value	5	32	133
Dividends	3	7	122

Reproduced from Block (1999), Financial Analysts Journal, with permission from the Association for Investment Management and Research.

The most obvious way of ensuring that cash flows are central to an analyst's approach is to focus on valuation methodologies that put cash flow centre stage. However, as we have already mentioned the discounted cash flow methodology has been widely discredited due to its bastardization by sell-side analysts. Newer methodologies (which are in fact variants on DCF), such as economic value added (EVA) and cash flow return on investment (CFROI), are helping to put cash flow on the analyst's agenda.

EVA is simply the modern trendy name for the age-old concept of economic profit. Anyone who has sat through Capital Budgeting 101 knows that net present value (NPV) is the correct way in which to evaluate an investment project (DCF is, of course, an NPV). EVA is nothing more than a method of implementing NPV. The economic profit is compared to the cost of capital, if it exceeds this cost of capital, then it is judged a sound investment.

In contrast, CFROI is an internal rate of return (IRR)-based measure. CFROI measures the return on investment expected over the average life of the firm's existing assets. The firm has made current and past investment decisions that should generate future cash flows. CFROI is the return that equates the gross cash investment with the sum of the present value of the annual gross cash flow and the present value of the terminal value. To enhance value, firms should increase the spread between CFROI and the cost of capital.

Note that DCF, EVA and CFROI have many elements in common. In particular they require that some measure of present value is compared against a cost of capital. It is to this element of the valuation conundrum that we now turn, and investigate from a behavioural perspective.

4.5 COST OF CAPITAL

In our cost of capital we will focus exclusively on the cost of equity. The cost of debt is a far less controversial area. Most equity analysts use something like the following to calculate their discount factors:

$$\text{Discount factor} = \text{Risk-free rate} + \beta \text{ (market equity risk premium)}$$

where β is derived from a capital asset pricing model (CAPM). We will leave aside the question of how to determine the market equity risk premium for the time being; that will be covered in Chapter 6 on asset allocation. For the purposes of our discussion here, we will focus on the other elements of the cost of equity capital.

4.5.1 Capital Asset Pricing Model

Notice how glibly we slip CAPM into the conversation. But in actuality the estimation of β is fraught with difficulties. The issues created by moving from the theory of CAPM to actually calculating estimates are frequently ignored by practitioners, yet they are non-trivial in nature. CAPM requires the estimation of the following regression:

$$r_{i,t} - r_{f,t} = \beta_i(r_{m,t} - r_{f,t}) + \mu_t$$

where:

$r_{i,t}$ = return on stock i during period t
$r_{f,t}$ = risk-free rate during period t
$r_{m,t}$ = return on the market portfolio during period t
β_i = beta coefficient to be estimated
μ_t = a random error term

Firstly, CAPM requires us to use the market portfolio ... but translating that notion into a measurable variable is exceptionally difficult. Most common sources of β simply take a leading domestic index such as the S&P500, or the FTSE 100, as the market portfolio with little or no thought as to the bias that may be introduced by such a selection (this is the celebrated Roll critique). Bartholdy and Pearce (2001) show that estimates of the equity risk premium may be up to 1% different using monthly data depending on the index used as a proxy for the market portfolio. In addition they demonstrate the wide variety of βs that can be generated depending on the index chosen as the market portfolio (Table 4.4).

Secondly, a choice over the observation period must be made. Should the data be daily, weekly or monthly. Then a decision over the sample period must be overcome. Is five years of monthly data better or worse than 260 weeks of weekly returns?

The fourth decision concerns the estimation procedure. Ordinary least squares is frequently used, however, when daily data on thinly traded stocks is utilized complex correction methods such as Scholes–Williams or Dimson estimators may be more appropriate. Finally, a decision over whether or not a shrinkage factor should be applied must be made. Many sources of beta choose to use two thirds of the estimated beta, plus one third of the market beta (1.0) — effectively drawing the estimate back towards 1. The main justification for doing this seems to be that extreme events will dampen out over time, leading β_i to converge to 1.

It should also be noted that as Fama and MacBeth (1973) showed, beta was much easier to estimate at the portfolio level than at the stock level. Stock level βs change over time as size, leverage and the risk of the business change. Portfolio βs are more stable over time, and generally have a lower residual variance than single-stock βs.

Because of these serious estimation issues, some CAPM defenders say it is untestable, and hence cannot be shown to be wrong. Whilst this is theoretically true, practitioners are forced to make decisions that allow them to estimate betas. Bartholdy and Pearce (2001) find that five years of monthly data, with an equally weighted index as a proxy for the market portfolio, seems to offer the most efficient estimation of β.

Table 4.4 Range of estimated β

Index	Average β	Standard deviation
S&P	1.09	0.47
MSCI	0.97	0.51
CRSP value weighted	1.11	0.48
CRSP equally weighted	0.92	0.47

Source: Bartholdy and Pearce (2001).

4.5.2 Experimental Evidence on CAPM

One interesting line of research is being conducted by Peter Bossaerts at CalTech (see Bossaerts, 2001). He points out that we may be being very ambitious in trying to test CAPM by looking at real-world markets. He has pioneered the use of experimental markets to test CAPM. After all in an experimental market, the market portfolio is known with certainty (by design) in contrast to the real world. So far the experiments have been few and far between and offer mixed evidence on the usefulness of CAPM.

One word of caution, Bossaerts' subjects are all familiar with standard financial theory, and therefore the experiments may well be biased towards finding support for CAPM. As we saw with the experiments on Keynes' beauty contest, the outcomes may well be sensitive to the nature of the subject pool. Give a group of game theorists a beauty contest, and the Nash equilibrium of zero is much more likely to be found than if the same contest is conducted amongst the readers of the financial press. The same could well be true of these experimental asset markets — economists may have a tendency towards CAPM, investors may not.

4.5.3 Empirical Evidence on CAPM

The very early tests of CAPM such as Lintner (1965) were not a resounding success. If you plot or regress average returns against individual stock βs, you find a lot of dispersion, and little evidence of a relationship. However, when Fama and MacBeth (1973) decided to use portfolios rather than individual stocks, a clear relationship between β and returns was uncovered, just as predicted by the theory. CAPM was heralded as *the* asset pricing model.

In 1981, Banz uncovered the first serious challenge to the CAPM when he found that small stocks seemed to outperform large stocks regardless of their βs. This is a clear violation of the efficient markets basis for CAPM, after all under CAPM β is all you need to assess the 'riskiness' of a stock (or portfolio).

A warning signal should flash in as much as the small cap effect has essentially not been seen for the last decade or so. Indeed, Horowitz, Loughran and Savin (2000) show that using a wide variety of techniques, there is no evidence of a small cap effect in the period 1980–1996 for the US market. This immediately suggests that we may not be capturing a 'true' risk factor but rather picking up some odd preference for small caps in the 1970s/1980s, or alternatively a surge in demand for large caps in the 1990s. This was exactly the argument we made in the previous chapter when discussing the life cycle of an investment style.

A second 'anomaly' is the well-documented value effect. That is the pronounced tendency for stocks with low price to book value (value stocks) to outperform the high price to book stocks (growth/glamour stocks). This is, of course, the subject matter of the previous chapter in which we discussed style investing. However, once again it should be borne in mind that if some market participants follow positive feedback investment strategies, then it becomes virtually impossible to define the true mean return for a style. We could have just been witnessing a fad for value on a long-term basis, rather than a true risk factor.

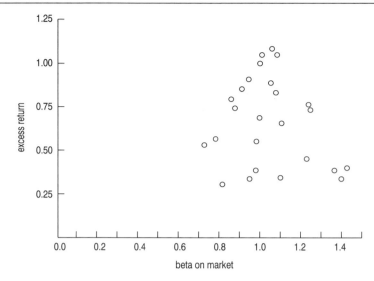

Figure 4.6 Average returns vs. market beta for 25 stock portfolios sorted on size and book to market

Reproduced from Cochrane, J.; Asset Pricing. Copyright © 2001. Reprinted by permission of Princeton University Press.

Figure 4.6 shows the value size puzzle. It covers US stocks between 1947 and 1996, with the NYSE used as a proxy for the market portfolio. The stocks have been sorted into portfolios based on size and book/market ratios. The mean return to each of these portfolios is plotted on the vertical axis, with the portfolio beta plotted on the horizontal axis. As can clearly be seen, the highest performing portfolios have average returns three times higher than the lowest portfolios, and this variation is unrelated to the portfolios' betas.

Cochrane (2001) digs a little deeper to explore these violations of CAPM. The next two Figures (4.7 and 4.8) connect portfolios that have different size within the same book/market category, and different book/market within the same size category. Variation in size (within a given book/market class) produces a variation in average returns that is positively related to β estimates. However, variation in book/market (within a given size class) produces a variation in average returns that is actually negatively associated with estimated βs! No wonder that CAPM looks like such a disaster when confronted with portfolios such as these.

4.5.4 The Assumptions of CAPM

Like all good economists, I was trained to judge a model by its predictions not its assumptions. However, when a model fails empirically as spectacularly as CAPM seems to have done, then it is time to turn to the assumptions that underlie the model and assess their validity.

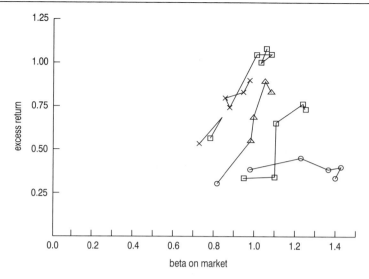

Figure 4.7 Average excess returns vs. market beta. Lines connect portfolios with different size category within book/market categories

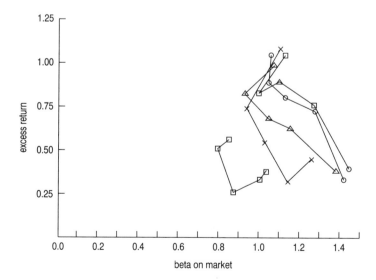

Figure 4.8 Average excess returns vs. market beta. Lines connect portfolios with different book/market categories within size categories

CAPM assumes:

   I. No transaction costs — i.e. no commission and no bid–offer spreads.
  II. Investors can take any position (long or short) in any stock in any size without affecting the market price.
 III. No taxes — hence investors are indifferent between dividends and capital gains.
  IV. Investors are risk-averse.
   V. Investors share a common time horizon.
  VI. Investors view stocks only in mean–variance space.
 VII. Investors control risk through diversification.
VIII. All assets, including human capital, can be bought and sold on the market.
  IX. Investors can lend and borrow at the risk-free rate.

None of these assumptions fits well with the reality of financial markets. In fact, the first two chapters are really a detailed critique of how and why these assumptions are so wrong. So it comes as little wonder to us that CAPM is flawed, even leaving aside the practical issues of problematic implementation. If the assumptions that make CAPM work are broken, no wonder it doesn't work as an empirical tool.

Karceski (2000) relates the rise of the institutional investing and the returns chasing behaviour to the death of β more generally. He posits that investors chase returns through time, precipitating unusually large aggregate chase flows into mutual funds just after a dramatic run up in the stock market. They also chase returns in the cross-section — that is to say each period the mutual funds compete to capture the largest share of aggregate inflows, with the best performing mutual fund attracting the highest inflow.

These flow dynamics induce an asymmetry such that fund managers care most about outperforming their peers during bull markets (when the rewards to outperformance are highest). Since high β stocks tend to outperform the broad market when the general market rises, active fund managers will tilt their portfolios towards high β stocks — reducing the expected return in equilibrium, and hence reducing the relationship between β and stock returns.

It is noteworthy that early studies showed risk was well captured by β. However, later studies discredited the single-factor risk model comprehensively. The timing of these findings, with the modern studies falling in the post-1980 period, coincides with the rapid expansion of the mutual fund industry (see Table 4.5).

Table: 4.5   The rise of institutional investors

Year	Total equity held by institutional investors (%)
1950	6.1
1970	26.7
1990	44.1
1998	49.6

4.5.5 Multifactor Models

The empirical regularity of the small cap effect, and the value effect, has led to their inclusion in the next generation of asset pricing models. In 1993, Fama and French (two of the staunch efficient market stalwarts) proposed a three-factor model for asset pricing (Fama and French, 1996 gives an excellent summary of their work in this area). The Fama–French three-factor model (FF3 hereafter) is an extension of the original CAPM style approach. In addition to the excess market return of the standard CAPM, FF3 adds the return on small stocks minus the return on big stocks (SMB, in the literature), and also the return on value stocks minus the return on growth stocks (HML, high minus low book/market).

The FF3 model can therefore be written as:

$$r_{i,t} - r_{f,t} = \beta_i(r_{m,t} - r_{f,t}) + \delta_i(\text{SMB}_i) + \phi(\text{HML}_t) + \mu_t$$

The Fama–French factors are constructed using the six value-weighted portfolios formed on size and book-to-market. These portfolios, which are constructed at the end of each June, from 1926 to 2000, are the intersections of two portfolios formed on size (market equity, ME) and three portfolios formed on the ratio of book equity to market equity (BE/ME). The size breakpoint for year t is the median NYSE market equity at the end of June of year t. BE/ME for June of year t is the book equity for the last fiscal year end in $t - 1$ divided by ME for December of $t - 1$. The BE/ME breakpoints are the 30th and 70th NYSE percentiles:

Median ME

	Small value	Big value
70th BE/ME percentile ———	Small neutral	Big neutral
30th BE/ME percentile ———	Small growth	Big growth

The portfolios for July of year t to June of $t + 1$ include all NYSE, AMEX and NASDAQ stocks for which we have market equity data for December of $t - 1$ and June of t, and (positive) book equity data for $t - 1$.

SMB (small minus big) is the average return on the three small portfolios minus the average return on the three big portfolios:

$$\text{SMB} = 1/3 \,(\text{Small value} + \text{Small neutral} + \text{Small growth})$$

$$- 1/3 \,(\text{Big value} + \text{Big neutral} + \text{Big growth})$$

HML (high minus low) is the average return on the two value portfolios minus the average return on the two growth portfolios:

$$\text{HML} = 1/2 \,(\text{Small value} + \text{Big value}) - 1/2 \,(\text{Small growth} + \text{Big growth})$$

$r_m - r_f$, the excess return on the market, is the value-weighted return on all NYSE, AMEX and NASDAQ stocks (from CRSP) minus the one month Treasury bill rate (from Ibbotson Associates).

4.5.6   Source of Multifactor Models: Efficient Markets View: Risk-based

FF3 has much more success in explaining asset pricing than the standard CAPM. However debate rages over what FF3 actually represents. To the efficient marketeers it is obvious that only risk can be priced in equilibrium, and therefore SMB and HML must represent some risk that *all* investors fear. If only a subgroup fear the risk, then it can't be priced in equilibrium, rather the two groups will trade until each has the desired level of exposure to the particular risk factor in question.

However, HML doesn't appear to be well correlated with standard indicators of financial distress. The best hope for the believers in efficient markets is found in a series of papers by Vassalou (Vassalou, 2000; Liew and Vassalou, 2000; etc.). She attempts to link SMB and HML to movements in the economy, specifically GDP. Vassalou finds some evidence that SMB and HML are capable of forecasting movements in GDP (much like the slope of the yield curve). However, as we point out below, other samples cast doubt on the equilibrium nature of SMB and HML.

4.5.7   Source of Multifactor Models: Non-risk-based

Surely one of the most important elements of an equilibrium asset pricing model is constancy in its factors. That is SMB and HML should always proxy the fundamental risk. However, as we have already noted the disappearance of the small cap effect in the 1990s doesn't bode well for this approach.

Further damage is generated by Bossaerts and Fohlin (2000). They examine the cross-section of average annual returns on German common stock in the period 1881– 1913. They find beta is hardly important, and its explanatory power is swamped by size and the ratio of book value to market value. However, the HML portfolio has the opposite sign to that found in modern data — growth stocks outperform value stocks. SMB appears to be a product of sample selection bias, and disappears as a meaningful measure by the end of the sample. These kinds of non-constancies don't sit well with an equilibrium asset pricing model.

Of course, there is an alternative ... that the FF3 model is picking up some non-risk factors. MacKinlay (1995) reminds us that it is always possible to find a set of variables that will generate a good within-sample fit in an asset pricing model. However, these could easily be the result of data-snooping rather than fundamental risk characteristics. MacKinlay points out that the return to a factor must be proportional to its ability to forecast the future if the risk-based view is correct. Using squared Sharpe ratios, MacKinlay goes on to show that the deviations from CAPM are just too large to be accounted for by multifactor risk-based models.

Daniel and Titman (1997, etc.) explore a related argument in a series of papers. They seek to answer the question, is it characteristics (non-risk-based elements) or covariances (risk-based elements) that drive the FF3? As an example of their methodology consider the following: What is the value of a degree in terms of future earnings power? It is a fact that people with degrees earn more than people without degrees. But why? Does having a degree enhance earnings power (characteristic) or does it reflect a high IQ which is actually valued (factor/covariance)?

In order to tell these hypotheses apart, we need to look at the people with high IQ without degrees, and people with low IQ with degrees. If the characteristic explanation is true, then people with low IQ and degrees should still earn more. If the factor/covariance explanation is true, then people with high IQ but without degrees should earn more.

How do we relate this to FF3? Well we need to find value stocks that look like growth stocks, and growth stocks that look like value stocks! In order to find such stocks, Daniel and Titman sort the universe by book/market, split into deciles, then sort by factor loadings (ϕ from the FF3) to see how much each co-varies with HML.

In order to test the hypotheses, they form two net zero investment portfolios: one with zero factor loading but unbalanced in terms of book/market (long high book/market, short low book/market), this portfolio is called factor balance. The other portfolio has zero characteristics, that is equally matched in terms of book/market, but a high factor loading (high ϕ from FF3), this is called the characteristic balance portfolio.

If the factor/covariance model were correct then the factor balance portfolio should have approximately zero average return, and the characteristic balance portfolio should have high and positive return. On the other hand, if the characteristic model is correct then the characteristic balance portfolio should have an approximately zero average return, but the factor balance portfolio should have a high and positive return.

Daniel and Titman find that on US data, the characteristic balance portfolio has a roughly zero average return, and the factor balance portfolio has a significant positive return. That is to say, value stocks earn a premium even if they produce a pattern of returns like growth stocks, or a stock's expected return is determined by whether it has a high or low book/market (characteristic) rather than its return pattern (whether it co-varies with high or low book/market stocks). This clearly indicates that the characteristic model is a more powerful driver than the covariance (or risk-based) approach.

4.5.8 Sources of Multifactor Models: The Behavioural View

However, we still don't know if we are dealing with data-snooping or market inefficiencies. Black (1986) argued that it was impossible to discriminate between the hypothesis on the basis of realized (ex post) returns alone. Shefrin and Statman (1998) come up with a clever way of using expectations about returns and realized returns to distinguish between the various hypotheses.

They set out three hypotheses:

 I. Data-snooping
 II. Risk-based
III. Cognitive errors by investors

Their testing strategy is to see how both realized returns and expectations about returns are related to the factors of FF3. If data-snooping was the likely cause of the FF3 model, then we would expect realized returns to be correlated to the factors, but expectations about returns to be unrelated to the factors.

If the risk-based explanation for FF3 were true then we would expect similar correlations in the realized returns and the expectations about returns. If book/market (HML) is positively correlated with both realized returns and expectations about returns then risk is the driving factor. Investors require (expect) a high book/market to compensate them for risk, and they get it.

If cognitive errors are to blame for the FF3, we would expect realized returns and expectations about returns to have opposite signs. That is investors expect a high return from a low book/market stock (growth), but in fact they generally fail to receive it.

Using data on expectations about returns gathered from First Call and from Fortune surveys, Shefrin and Statman unearth the relationships outlined in Table 4.6. This is, of course, the pattern associated with investors making errors in their expectations. So for example, they constantly expect 'growth' stocks to outperform but are generally disappointed. This is a far cry from the efficient market interpretation of FF3. Could it be that FF3 is really a behavioural beta?

Remember that beta is defined relative to the market portfolio. Roll's critique is that the market portfolio is unknown, so beta can never be tested. However, could the FF3 be an attempt to correct the proxy used for market mispricing? If the market is inefficient, and we saw plenty of examples of this in Chapters 2 and 3, then the market proxy will need to be corrected for any mispricing. A behavioural beta will tilt the benchmark portfolio in the direction of the underpriced security, and away from the overpriced security.

Could this be why size and book-to-price create factors that influence realized returns? Both HML and SMB would seem to have this effect (see Shefrin and Statman, 1994 and Daniel, Hirschleifer and Subrahmanyam, 1999b for the theory and evidence respectively).

The debate over the source of FF3 factors is not some ivory tower debate, it has major implications for the way in which we value equities. Before we discuss these, there are some other potential factors for inclusion in an asset pricing model that need to be covered.

4.5.9 Momentum

The most high profile failure of the FF3 is its inability to explain momentum returns. This is the tendency for stocks that have outperformed to continue to outperform over a 3–12 month period by around 1% per month (Jegadeesh and Titman, 1993). See Table 4.7.

Table 4.6   Realized returns vs. expected returns

Factor	Realized return	Expectations about returns
Size (SMB)	Positive	Negative
Book/market (HML)	Positive	Negative

Table 4.7   US momentum effects

Time period	Average monthly return (%)
01/31–02/63	0.38
07/63–12/93	1.31
01/90–01/97	1.01

The efficient market approach has a particularly hard time dealing with momentum. Of course, a winner minus losers (WML) portfolio can be formed, but it is so blatantly ad hoc that just about everyone agrees it does not belong in an equilibrium asset pricing model.

It could of course be the result of data-snooping. However, Jegadeesh and Titman (1999) compare behavioural and data-snooping explanations of momentum. These two explanations have very different implications for patterns of returns post portfolio formation. The behavioural models specify that the holding period returns arise because of a delayed over-reaction to information that pushes the prices of winners (losers) above (below) their long-term values. These models predict that the returns of losers should exceed the returns of winners subsequent to the holding period. In contrast, the data-snooping explanation (Conrad and Kaul, 1998) suggests that the higher returns of winners in the holding period represent their unconditional expected rates of return and thus predict that the post-formation returns of the momentum portfolio will be positive on average in any post-ranking period. Jegadeesh and Titman

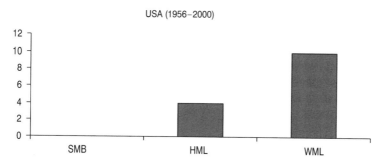

Figure 4.9   Size, style and momentum — US
Source: DKWR.

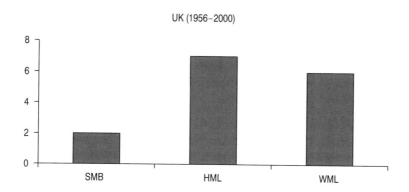

Figure 4.10   Size, style and momentum — UK
Source: DKWR.

find clear evidence of eventual reversal, as predicted by the behavioural models. This is exactly the pattern we used when we explored style rotation in the previous chapter. See Figures 4.9 and 4.10.

4.6   FACTORS FROM LIMITED ARBITRAGE

So far we have stressed the factors that affect stock returns from a behavioural perspective. However, there are two potential factors that may be driven by limited arbitrage rather than behavioural traits themselves. It is to these factors that we now turn.

4.6.1   Idiosyncratic Risk

One of the fundamental tenets of CAPM is that investors diversify risk across their portfolios. Hence they are left only with some desired gearing (β) of the market level of risk. If that fails to occur (and we showed in Chapter 1 that investors are dreadful at diversifying) then idiosyncratic risk may start to matter for asset pricing.

In addition, as we showed in Chapter 2, the financing risks faced by arbitrageurs mean that they can't afford to worry only about price movements in the long term, but rather they are forced to concern themselves with intermediate price movements. From the minute the trade is put on, arbitrageurs are worried in case the price moves against them, they face margin calls, etc. This means that once again idiosyncratic risk starts to matter for asset prices.

Campbell *et al.* (2001) show that idiosyncratic risk has been rising. In fact stock-specific risk has doubled from its levels in the 1960s. They also show that market-level volatility has essentially been trendless over the same time period. So the rise in idiosyncratic risk must have been accompanied by a fall in the average pairwise correlation between stocks. In fact Campbell *et al.* show that the average pairwise correlation amongst US equities is only around one third of its level in the 1960s. See Figures 4.11–4.13.

Aside from asset pricing issues, these trends have major implications for portfolio construction. Most finance textbooks report that optimal portfolio diversification (i.e. dropping the portfolio's risk profile to be equal to the risk of the overall index) requires around 10–15 stocks. However, the studies that produced these numbers were carried out in the 1960s.

Campbell *et al.* paint a very different picture when the correlation statistics are updated. Between 1974 and 1985, you would have needed to hold more like 20 stocks within your portfolio to ensure that you were completely diversified. Between 1996 and 1997, the required number of stocks has soared, such that you would need to hold around 50 stocks in order to achieve comparable levels of risk reduction.

4.6.2   Why Should Individual Stock Volatility be Rising?

Three potential explanations for this trend can be uncovered. Firstly, the death of the conglomerate. Firms trading across multiple product lines tend to have lower stock market values than portfolios of specialized firms in the same industries (see Chapter 7 for more details) — diversification by corporates is punished by investors. This

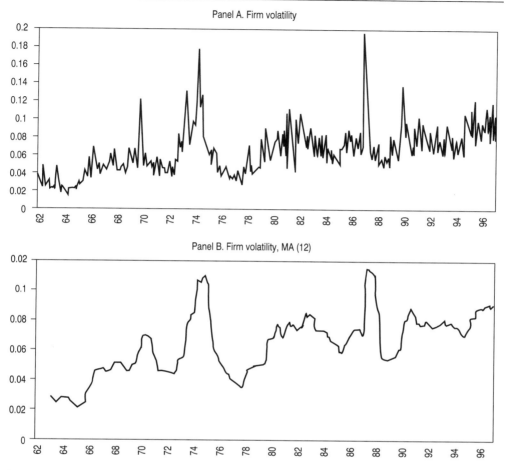

Annualized firm-level volatility FIRM. The top panel shows the annualized variance within each month of daily firm returns relative to the firm's industry, calculated for the period July 1962 to December 1977. The bottom panel shows a backwards 12-month moving average of FIRM. NBER-dated recessions are shaded in grey to illustrate cyclical movements in volatility.

Figure 4.11   Idiosyncratic risk

Source: Campbell *et al.* (2001). Reproduced from Blackwell Publishers.

encourages firms to focus on their core competencies and niche markets. These 'small' focused firms are by their very nature subject to more idiosyncratic risk than large conglomerates.

A second potential cause of increased, idiosyncratic volatility is the speeding up of the firm's life cycle. Equity markets are increasingly coming to resemble venture capital markets. Firms are coming to the market at a far earlier stage of development than in the past. According to Professor Jay Ritter in 1997, 68% of firms listing on the US market had track records covering 12 months of earnings. In 1999, this had fallen to

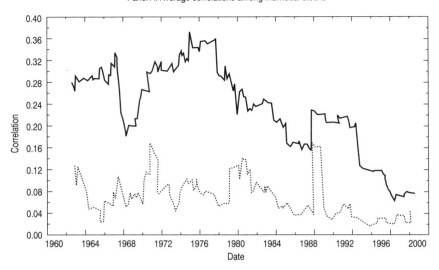

Figure 4.12 Average pairwise correlation

Source: Campbell *et al.* (2001). Reproduced from Blackwell Publishers.

Average correlations and R^2 statistics of market model for individual stocks. The top panel reports the equally weighted average pairwise correlation across stocks traded on the NYSE, AMEX, and Nasdaq. The solid line is the average correlation over the past 60 months of monthly data, and the dotted line is the average correlation over the past 12 months of daily data. The bottom panel reports the equally weighted average R^2 statistic of a market model, estimated using the past 60 months of monthly data (solid line) or the past 12 months of daily data (dotted line). Stocks included in the calculation at each point in time are required to have a complete return history over the past 60 months (solid line) or 12 months (dotted line).

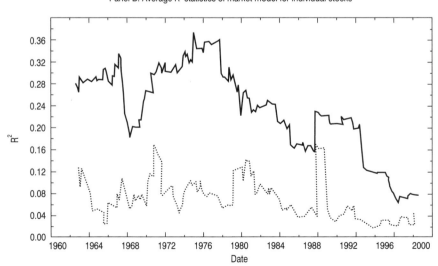

Figure 4.13 Average R^2 of market model for individual stocks

Source: Campbell *et al.* (2001). Reproduced from Blackwell Publishers.

just 25% of firms listing. The anxiety this causes investors translates directly into volatility.

Malkiel and Xu (2000a) make an associated point. The rise in growth stocks may have driven the rise in stock-specific risk. Growth stocks tend to be small highly focused firms with products in specialized markets. By their very nature growth stocks are likely to have a far higher degree of idiosyncratic risk. Indeed Malkiel and Xu show that idiosyncratic risk is positively related to long-term earnings growth forecasts (Figure 4.14).

A third potential cause is likely to be the speeding up of the entire financial system. In the latter part of the 1990s, automated dealing, combined with highly active fund managers, and increasing numbers of day traders and the like have combined to exacerbate price trends to an unprecedented level.

The degree to which idiosyncratic risk matters for asset pricing is an empirical question. Malkiel and Xu produced the chart shown in Figure 4.15 to illustrate the high degree of linkage between excess returns (after an FF3 model has been applied) and idiosyncratic volatility. This clearly suggests that in any model of equity returns we should give considerable attention to including a proxy for aggregate idiosyncratic risk.

4.6.3 Liquidity

When we were discussing failures of the law of one price in the context of the bond market in Chapter 2, one recurring theme was investors' quest for liquidity. In equity

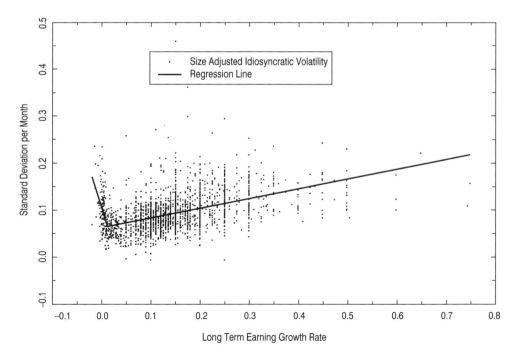

Figure 4.14 Idiosyncratic risk and forecast long-term growth
Source: Malkiel and Xu (2000a).

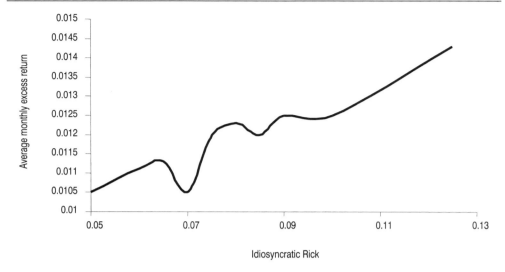

Figure 4.15 Idiosyncratic risk and returns
Source: Malkiel and Xu (2000a).

markets with limited arbitrage, liquidity also matters. Liquidity is a slightly nebulous concept but generally denotes the ability to trade in large quantities quickly, at low cost and without moving the price.

Turning the concept of liquidity into measurable variables presents itself as an embarrassment of riches. Chorida, Roll and Subrahmanyam (2000a,b) form daily time series of various measures of liquidity such as depth and quoted and effective bid–ask spreads, and also trading volume such as dollar and share volume. Jones (2000) collects an annual time series of average quoted bid–ask spreads. Amihud (2000) constructs an annual aggregate liquidity measure by averaging across NYSE stocks the ratios of average absolute price change trading volume. Lo and Wang (2000) use an average turnover variable as their liquidity proxy. Pastor and Stambaugh (2001) use a more complex measure based on order flow (Figure 4.16). However, the good news for practitioners is that essentially all the various estimates point in the same direction.

Pastor and Stambaugh (2001) is a particularly important study because it sets out to discover if liquidity risk is priced in equities. In order to test this hypothesis they calculate sensitivity, denoted for stock i by its liquidity beta βL_i, the slope coefficient on L_t (their aggregate liquidity index) in a multiple regression in which the other independent variables are additional factors considered important for asset pricing. To investigate whether the stock's expected return is related to βL_i, they follow a straightforward portfolio-based approach to create a universe of assets whose liquidity betas are sufficiently disperse. At the end of each year, starting with 1965, they sort stocks based on their predicted values of βL_i and form 10 portfolios. The post-formation returns on these portfolios during the next 12 months are linked across years to form a single return series for each decile portfolio. The excess returns on those

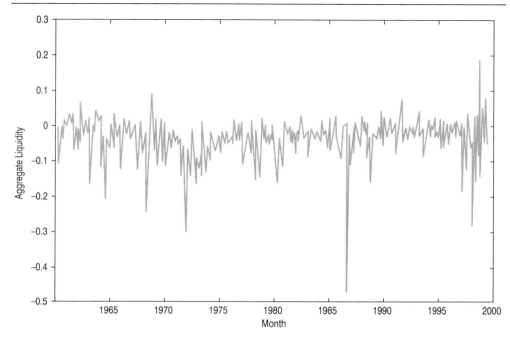

Aggregate liquidity. Each month's observation is constructed by averaging individual-stock measures for the month and then multiplying by (m_t/m_1), where m_t is the total dollar value at the end of month $t - 1$ of the stocks included in the average in month t, and month 1 corresponds to August 1962. An individual stock's measure for a given month is a regression slope coefficient estimated using daily returns and volume data within that month. Tick marks correspond to July of the given year.

Figure 4.16   Pastor and Stambaugh's liquidity measure

Source: Pastor and Stambaugh (2001).

portfolios are then regressed on return-based factors that are commonly used in empirical asset pricing studies. To the extent that the regression intercepts, or alphas, differ from zero, βL_i explains a component of expected returns not captured by exposures to the other factors.

Pastor and Stambaugh use both FF3, and FF3 plus WML (a momentum portfolio). They find that stocks' liquidity betas play an important role in asset pricing. Stocks with higher liquidity betas exhibit higher returns. In particular, they find a spread between the top and bottom deciles of predicted liquidity betas produces an abnormal return (alpha) of 7.5% per year with respect to FF3 plus WML, and over 9% per year with respect to FF3.

Liquidity clearly matters for asset pricing. Yet despite this, analysts give scant attention to the subject. Instead discussions of liquidity are usually centred within fund management groups, trading desks and derivative desks. More thought needs to be given to understanding liquidity if analysts are to become more useful to investors.

4.6.4 Use Matters

Whether or not the factors outlined above result from the efficient pricing of risk, data-snooping or behavioural bias and limited arbitrage matters for investors may seem like a dry academic debate, but it is actually vital to grasp the importance of the drivers behind stock valuation.

As we already noted, if the market is efficiently pricing risk, investors can do no better than hold a linear combination of these tracking portfolios. However, if they result from behavioural biases and limited arbitrage then higher returns are potentially possible.

From an analyst's point of view, the difference between risk- and non-risk-based drivers of valuation is key. If the sources of the multiple factors are risk-based, then they need to incorporate them into their cost of capital calculations for fundamental value. However, if the sources are behavioural biases and limited arbitrage then we find a separation between fundamental value and market value (or what prices *should* be and what prices actually *are*). If we are interested in pure fundamental value (perhaps for corporate finance reasons) then CAPM generated βs are likely to be the optimal method for cost of equity calculations. However, most analysts are also interested (or at least should be interested) in what determined the market price. In order to estimate this, then a multifactor model such as:

$$r_{i,t} - r_{f,t} = \beta_i(r_{m,t} - r_{f,t}) + \delta_i(\text{SMB}_t) + \phi(\text{HML}_t) + \eta(\text{WML}_t) + \rho(\text{IDVOL}_t)$$
$$+ \omega(\text{LIQUID}) + \mu_t$$

where:

$r_{m,t} - r_{f,t}$ = the market equity risk premium
SMB = the return on small minus large cap stocks
HML = the return of value minus growth stocks
WML = the return on winners minus losers (momentum)
IDVOL = the idiosyncratic risk component
LIQUID = a measure of aggregate market liquidity

should be used. Or perhaps a model based on characteristics directly such as price to book and market capitalization, and past momentum rather than how the return co-varies with the factor portfolios (as suggested by Daniel and Titman's work).

Stein (1996) explores these issues from a corporates perspective. If this kind of model is based on irrational market behaviour then managers need to choose the capital budgeting method that suits them. For instance, if managers want to maximize short-term share prices, then they should use a model that reflects these factors, i.e. a multifactor model. If, on the other hand, managers want to maximize long-run value, then an estimate of fundamental asset risk (such as CAPM β) should be used.

This dichotomy leads to clear predictions: fundamental asset risk measures (such as CAPM β) will be used by firms with strong balance sheets, or the availability of debt; whereas firms with a need to frequently approach the market are much more likely to use multifactor models. For instance, cash strapped dot.coms should have investments that respond more sensitively to movements in the share price than AAA rated utility with a balance sheet laden with assets.

As an example, consider two airlines — one financially constrained, the other not so. Assume a wave of negative sentiment hits the airline sector, stock prices fall, and hence expected returns rise. The constrained firm using its multifactor discount rate must raise its hurdle rate for investment. The unconstrained firm using a fundamental asset risk approach will leave its hurdle rate unchanged. The constrained firm may be forced to sell assets (planes) to its rivals. This, of course, is an example of an asset fire sale as discussed in Chapter 2.

Conversely, if a positive wave of sentiment hits the airline sector, and prices rise, so expected returns drop, the firm using the multifactor model will lower its discount/hurdle rate, and start buying planes — potentially overinvesting on the back of sentiment. Pulvino (1998) documents exactly this kind of pattern of asset purchasing and sales in the airline industry.

4.7   AN ANALYST'S GUIDE

By way of a summary for analysts here are the main points covered in this chapter:

   I. Fundamentals aren't everything.
  II. Don't be too optimistic.
 III. Remember cash flows not earnings (check accruals).
 IV. Use absolute valuations (DCF) not relative.
  V. Use reverse engineered models.
 VI. Remember that most firms don't manage to sustain their competitive advantage (see Chapter 3).
 VII. Think carefully about the cost of capital.
VIII. Are you interested in fundamental or market prices?

Portfolio Construction and Risk Management

It is the part of a wise man to keep himself today for tomorrow, and not to venture all his eggs in one basket

Miguel de Cerantes Saavedra

Put all your eggs in one basket, and watch that basket

Mark Twain

5.1   INTRODUCTION

The disciplines of portfolio construction and risk management are intimately related, although not often associated together. In fact, both deal in variables and languages that are very close, if not identical. The focus of each area may be different, but the objects of study and the tools used are amazingly similar. Both are essentially concerned with some form of optimization. As such, correlations and covariances are at the heart of each practice.

Behavioural finance, and indeed the related study known as phynance (or econophysics) can greatly improve our understanding of the nature of both portfolio construction and risk management. By the nature of the subject matter, this chapter is more technically demanding (although no more mathematical) than other chapters. We have already touched on some implications of our approach to the practices of portfolio construction and risk management in Chapter 2 on limited arbitrage, and in Chapter 4 in terms of diversification benefits. However, in this chapter we seek to explore these issues more explicitly.

5.2   COVARIANCES

As mentioned in the previous chapter, Daniel and Titman (1998) show that the characteristics model performs better at predicting expected returns than the covariance model. That finding has important implications for portfolio construction and risk management.

As Cochrane (1999b) demonstrates so clearly, if expected returns are consistent with FF3 investors can do no better than hold a linear combination of the three factor portfolios. Any deviation from this combination will increase the portfolio's variance without increasing its expected return. This is a multidimensional extension of the classical results from modern portfolio theory on the fund separation theorem. Since we are no longer dealing with just one factor (β) it is not so simple to present graphically, but the intuition remains the same.

However, Daniel and Titman show that covariances are not directly linked to expected returns. This suggests that investors can build superior portfolios with mean variance optimizers that use characteristics to generate expected returns, with a separately estimated covariance matrix. Unlike the efficient markets view, there are gains to be made from more precise estimates of the covariance matrix.

Given that Daniel and Titman suggest there may be significant gains from modelling the covariance matrix, it is somewhat surprising that more effort isn't put into such enterprises. Expected returns attract massive amounts of attention from academics and practitioners alike, however, it is common practice to use historical estimates of variances, covariances and correlations — indeed all of the risk management industry is built around the use of historical estimates of variances, covariances and correlations.

Chan, Karceski and Lakonishok (1999) explore the possibilities of estimating the variance/covariance matrix and correlations using CAPM and FF3, plus a series of other models. As an example of just how important covariance estimators are in the portfolio optimization process, they set up an example where an investor is assumed to have perfect foresight (effectively he forecasts the future covariances perfectly). They also impose non-negativity constraints (no short selling) and a maximum weighting of 2% per stock in the portfolio. Each year this hypothetical investor selects the minimum variance portfolio from a set of 250 stocks randomly selected from the NYSE and AMEX markets. The experiment is repeated each year from 1973 to 1997. This strategy yields a portfolio with a standard deviation of 6.85%, while the benchmark (the equally weighted 250 randomly selected stocks) has a standard deviation that is more than twice as large (16.5%). Of course perfect foresight is a highly unrealistic assumption, but Chan, Karceski and Lakonishok find, when models are used to forecast the covariances, they still have lower standard deviations than the benchmark.

To investigate the forecasting ability of various models, Chan, Karceski and Lakonishok take a random sample of 250 stocks from the domestic equities listed on NYSE and AMEX from 1968 to 1997. The forecasts from the models are formed on the basis of 60 months of past data. At the end of April each year, each model's forecasts of covariances are compared to the realized sample covariances. Their tests reveal that simply extrapolating the past tends to lead to overfitting of the data. The forecasts offered by CAPM and FF3 are improvements over using historical numbers.

Effectively, the models tend to smooth out the data, leading to less extreme forecasts than pure extrapolation. In turn this generates smaller forecast errors. Interestingly, Chan, Karceski and Lakonishok find no gains from attempting to forecast correlations (Table 5.1). However, much attention needs to be devoted to investigating our ability to forecast risk as well as return.

Moskowitz (2001) uses a GARCH (generalized autoregressive conditional heteroskedasticity) to quantify the contribution made by each anomaly to contemporaneous and future covariance risk. He finds that the market portfolio (i.e. the equity risk premium) is the largest contributor to and forecaster of covariances. He also finds that anomalous returns associated with firm size (SMB) are closely linked to the covariance matrix, and indeed improved forecasting ability with respect to covariances. However, the returns associated with price to book (HML) and momentum (MOM) are unrelated to covariance risk.

Chen (2001) extends MacKinlay's (1995) work into a dynamic setting which we discussed in the previous chapter. The intertemporal CAPM Chen uses delivers two key features. A factor has to forecast future market returns to justify its risk premium. It may contain information about either future expected returns or future volatility, but its price of risk has to be linked to the amount of information that the factor contains

Table 5.1 Performance of covariance forecasting models

Properties Model	Mean	Standard deviation
Extrapolation	0.0027	0.0018
CAPM	0.0025	0.0014
FF3	0.0026	0.0015
Absolute forecast error Model	Mean	Median
Extrapolation	0.0040	0.0028
CAPM	0.0037	0.0026
FF3	0.0038	0.0027

Source: Adapted from Chan, Karceski and Lakonishok (1999).

about the future. Secondly, risk premia across factors must also be linked to the willingness of the economic agents to bear risk. Effectively Chen tests whether SMB, HML and MOM have any ability to forecast either returns or risks.

Using data covering April 1953 to December 1999, the estimates cannot reject the fact that there isn't any information content in these effects about forecasts of future returns or future volatility. However, when one imposes the constraint that their risk premia must be linked to each other by the representative agent's willingness to bear risk, the model rejects that HML and MOM are consistent with the implementation of the ICAPM developed here. However, SMB is not rejected by the model. Chen is effectively saying that size is roughly correctly priced by the market, but value/growth and momentum aren't equilibrium factors.

5.3 CORRELATIONS

As noted above, correlations are considerably harder to estimate and hence forecast. In part this is due to the asymmetric nature of correlations. There has long been a saying in financial markets that the only thing that goes up in a bear market is correlation. Table 5.2 shows the findings of Erb, Harvey and Viskanta (1994), who examine the correlation amongst equity markets under different market environments.

Erb, Harvey and Viskanta study the correlation of equity markets based on US dollar denominated returns for the MSCI indices on a monthly basis between January 1970 and December 1993. They rank the data on the basis of market conditions, and then estimate correlations for each sub-sample. The results show just how important asymmetric correlation can be. For instance, during periods when both the US and German markets are rising the correlation is just 8.6%, however, when both the US and German markets are falling the correlation jumps to 52%. This clearly demonstrates the power of the old market adage. Yet despite this clear violation of one of the key assumptions of modern portfolio theory (constant correlations), both portfolio constructors and risk managers continue to 'assume' constant correlation in order to estimate their models.

Table 5.2 Correlations amongst equity markets as a function of market environment

		Up–up	Down–down	Out-of-phase	Total
US	Germany	8.6	52	−61	35
	Japan	21	41	−54	26
	UK	32	58	−60	50
Germany	Japan	4.6	24	−47	40
	UK	22	40	−62	42
Japan	UK	12	21	−54	37

Adapted from Erb, Harvey and Viskanta (1994), Financial Analysts Journal, with permission from the Association for Investment Management and Research.

Recently, more evidence of asymmetries (or semi-correlations) has been uncovered by the likes of Longin and Solnik (2001) for the correlation between international markets and Ang and Chen (2001) for the correlation between individual stocks and the US market. Longin and Solnik point out that their findings using extreme value theory (more on this below) cannot be replicated via standard models of volatility used by risk managers such as GARCH.

Ang and Chen find that correlations conditional on 'downside' movements (when both a US equity portfolio and the US market fall) are on average 11.6% higher than implied by a normal distribution. In contrast, correlations conditional on 'upside' movements (when both an equity portfolio and the market rise) cannot be statistically distinguished from those implied by a normal distribution. Interestingly, Ang and Chen also find that small firms, value stocks and past losers tend to have higher asymmetric correlation than other stocks. In terms of industries the traditional defensive stocks such as utilities and petroleum companies tend to exhibit greater asymmetric correlation.

Nor is this a purely short-term phenomenon, Goetzmann, Li and Rouwenhorst (2001) examine no less than 150 years of data on the correlations amongst global equity markets. They find that the structure of global correlations shifts considerably through time. It is currently near an historical high — approaching levels of correlation last experienced during the Great Depression. Decomposing the pattern of correlation through time, Goetzmann, Li and Rouwenhorst find that roughly half the benefits of diversification available today to the international investor are due to the increasing number of world markets, and half due to lower than average correlation among the available markets.

Asymmetric correlations are important for several applications. For example, in optimal portfolio allocation, if all stocks tend to fall together as the market falls, the value of diversification may be overstated by those not taking the increase in downside correlations into account. Asymmetric correlations have similar implications in risk management.

Asymmetric correlations pose yet another challenge to the efficient markets view of the world. However, from our standpoint of irrational investors and limited arbitrage they are to be expected. As we saw in Chapter 2, the nature of limited arbitrage is that there are likely to be spillovers between assets due to the risks facing arbitrageurs. For instance, LTCM caused distortions on the Danish mortgage-backed asset market as it liquidated its positions, driven by events in Russia. So suddenly normally uncorrelated assets can easily develop very high correlations simply due to flows of funds (see Kyle and Wang, 1997 and Gromb and Vayanos, 2001 for theoretical models showing these features). Effectively, in these models correlations become endogenous.

Market participants have long known that correlations are endogenous. The most vivid example of endogenous correlations is the LTCM crisis of 1998. LTCM itself used a value-at-risk (VaR[1]) methodology as its risk control process. However, LTCM-style trades were being implemented by a large number of other market participants (for instance the arbitrage desk at Salomon, where LTCM was effectively born). They too all used VaR as a risk control process. When markets started to fall, driven by events in Russia, all the VaR models started to flash warning signals. This created a feedback loop, where investors tried to liquidate their positions, exacerbating already nervous market conditions. This is, of course, the asset fire sale that we discussed in Chapter 2.

In addition, models where investors are subject to loss aversion, such as Barberis, Huang and Santos (2000), could also give rise to asymmetric correlations. Remember from Chapter 1, that investors suffering from loss aversion treat gains and losses asymmetrically, and are very averse to downside risk (the empirical evidence suggests that people feel losses nearly twice as badly as they feel gains). So both elements of behavioural finance (irrational investors and limited arbitrage) suggest that we could expect to see asymmetric correlations.

To give an indication of the scale of the impact of asymmetric correlations on measures like VaR, Jorion (2000) cites the findings of Longin and Solnik (1985), who found that the correlation between national stock market indices was 0.12 higher in periods of market turbulence (it rose from 0.43 to 0.55). To see how this could bias a VaR calculation, consider a large diversified portfolio, under which the risk is proportional to the square root of the correlation. To correct for the asymmetric correlation, Jorion notes that the VaR estimate should be multiplied by $\sqrt{(0.55/0.43)} = 1.13$. A VaR that ignored the asymmetric correlation would understate the true risk by 13%! Thus asymmetric or endogenous correlations have a sizeable impact upon risk management practices. Despite the widespread acknowledgement of asymmetric and endogenous correlations from market participants, risk managers still routinely use historical correlations in their analysis.

Lest those who view the world in terms of sectors rather than countries think themselves immune from the pitfalls of asymmetric correlations and covariances, Table 5.3 shows that sectors are just as subject to different correlations under different market conditions. Once again, sectors are considerably more closely correlated during down–down phases of the market.

Although behavioural finance teaches us to expect to see such anomalies as asymmetric correlations and variances, the key question for practitioners must be can we actually use these insights to improve the optimization process, be it risk management or portfolio construction, or even asset allocation?

Gabbi (2001) shows that a neural network for predicting market returns performs quite well, at least in terms of market direction if not magnitude (i.e. the forecast is a

---

[1] Any reader wanting an introduction to VaR could do no better than read Philippe Jorion's masterful but very accessible book on the subject. Jorion (2000).

Table 5.3 Bull vs. bear correlations amongst sectors

World	Total corr.		Up–up corr.		Down–down corr.		Mixed corr.	
	Avg.	Vol.	Avg.	Vol.	Avg.	Vol.	Avg.	Vol.
Energy	47.65	27.19	71.58	8.88	79.03	10.39	−54.49	6.38
Materials	65.01	21.47	80.01	8.40	84.93	8.57	−53.61	9.95
Capital goods	86.20	8.01	88.79	5.38	93.23	4.18	−43.44	11.04
Commercial services and supply	70.94	10.99	81.82	4.37	81.57	11.16	−55.92	10.23
Transport	66.27	19.93	82.86	6.37	84.94	6.70	−56.64	10.88
Auto components	58.49	15.90	74.17	7.29	80.59	9.23	−55.48	6.59
Consumer durables and apparel	58.74	13.81	73.61	8.08	80.26	8.05	−53.96	9.17
Hotels, restaurants and leisure	67.00	12.46	78.40	6.38	83.74	7.44	−54.62	8.42
Media	79.34	9.46	82.34	8.66	90.17	4.94	−54.72	9.65
Retailing	70.06	18.14	80.61	9.23	85.72	6.05	−51.34	13.63
Food and drug retailing	60.79	19.79	76.06	7.80	82.46	9.04	−56.01	8.55
Food, beverages and tobacco	60.69	32.01	79.19	9.76	81.95	13.65	−54.28	11.30
Household and personal products	54.22	23.10	77.25	8.02	79.85	12.76	−54.95	11.27
Healthcare equipment and services	60.54	15.10	77.75	8.24	80.61	9.00	−62.63	8.10
Pharmaceuticals and biotechnology	68.02	24.85	80.11	10.47	86.19	10.18	−53.13	11.91
Banks	81.84	11.48	87.01	5.88	89.30	6.59	−46.86	16.92
Diverse financial	82.69	9.34	86.62	5.36	92.74	3.96	−45.48	8.84
Insurance	77.43	12.92	84.74	6.99	87.53	6.90	−49.27	13.62
Real estate	47.76	18.09	67.43	8.10	77.77	8.14	−52.73	6.86
Software and services	67.24	9.41	79.90	6.52	83.71	5.56	−47.23	9.85
Technical hardware and equipment	78.61	7.88	83.37	5.06	88.36	5.06	−52.68	11.58
Telecommunications services	77.66	7.10	82.59	6.65	89.15	4.86	−45.41	11.27
Utilities	64.35	17.91	79.05	8.65	83.64	8.25	−53.35	8.43

reasonable phase indicator of whether the markets under consideration are in an up–up, down–down or mixed phase). This phase indicator is a necessary input into a second neural network, which in turn predicts the asymmetric (or semi-) correlation. Gabbi finds that this method outperforms the more standard approach of assuming a constant correlation.

5.4 DISTRIBUTION OF RETURNS

Most readers will be familiar with the bell-shaped curve so beloved of statisticians — the normal distribution. However, as anyone who has looked at any financial data will know, the normal distribution is not a good proxy for the distribution of financial market returns. Figures 5.1 and 5.2 show the distribution of returns for a variety of stock markets, against a normal distribution.

They clearly show that the distribution of returns is non-normal. The normal distribution is symmetrical around the mean of the series. If a distribution is not symmetrical then it is said to be skewed. Negative skewness means that a distribution has a long left tail, and hence entails large negative values.

Just like asymmetric correlations and covariances can arise from models containing bounded rational agents and limits to arbitrage, so too can skewness arises naturally out of models that are based on behavioural finance. Hong and Stein (1999) analyse the implications of short sale constraints and differences of opinion on the higher moments. The intuition is relatively simple to understand. When a stock's price goes down, more information is revealed, specifically it reveals the level at which other investors will enter the market. We are effectively uncovering the valuations of those investors whose pessimistic views could not be initially revealed due to the short sale constraint. When the stock market goes up, the sidelined investors remain out of the market, and there is less information revealed. This increase in volatility after a downturn is the source of the skewness that we uncover in the data above.

One prediction of this approach is that stocks which investors disagree about more should exhibit greater skewness. Chen, Hong and Stein (2001) test this idea using increases in turnover as a sign of disagreement. They show that stocks whose turnover increases do indeed display greater subsequent skewness.

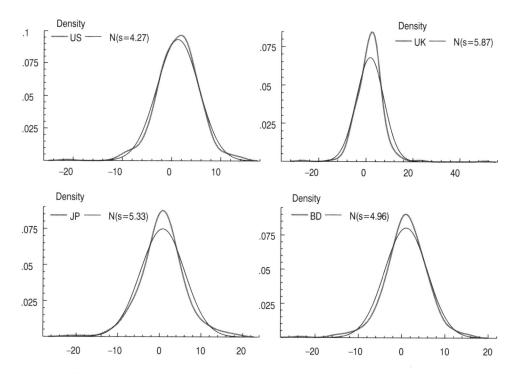

Figure 5.1 Distribution of stock market returns vs. normal distribution

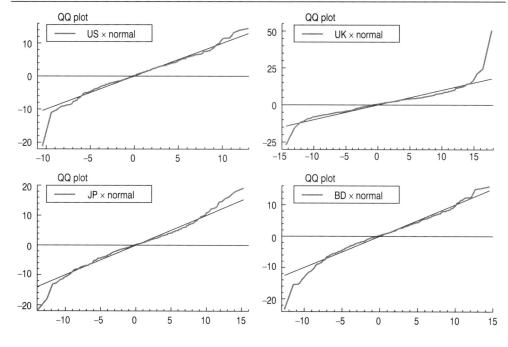

Figure 5.2   QQ plots

The other dimension that attracts an awful lot of attention is kurtosis. Kurtosis describes the degree of flatness of a distribution. The kurtosis of a normal distribution is 3. A kurtosis coefficient > 3 indicates that the tails decay less quickly than for the normal distribution, implying a greater likelihood of large values, positive and negative. See Table 5.4.

It is clear that all the markets exhibit so-called 'fat tails' (leptokurtosis, in the statistical jargon). These fat tails can be explained by two alternatives. The first view is that the true distribution is stationary and indeed does contain fat tails. The other view is that the distribution changes through time. As a result in times of turbulence, a stationary model could view large observations as outliers when they are really drawn from a distribution with temporarily greater dispersion.

Table 5.4   Kurtosis and skew in equity markets

Market	Skewness	Excess kurtosis
US	−0.4	2.4
UK	1.6	16.2
Japan	−0.01	1.8
Germany	−0.5	2.3

5.5   FAT TAILS OR OUTLIERS?

Risk management, portfolio optimization and tactical asset allocation all labour under the misguided view that crashes are just a result of the well-known fat tail observation. In this view, if we extrapolate the tail far enough then the risks will be captured.

However, Johansen and Sornette (1997, 2001a) show this to be a seriously flawed approach. In fact, far from lying in the fat tails of a distribution, crashes are actually generated from an entirely different distribution. One of the key lessons that both financial academics and practitioners can learn from physicists is to think more about scale.

In finance, we tend to take scale as given. We measure market moves over time horizons, be it minutes, hours, days or quarters, etc. We generally don't devote very much attention to the concept of scale. In physics (particularly statistical mechanics) scale is of vital importance, and researchers in the field give a great deal of time and thought to defining the scale which we want to use.

Johansen and Sornette point out that by using an arbitrary time frame, we may be missing some of the more important features of the system under consideration. They use a time-independent measure of market moves known as a draw down. These are cumulative market movements spread over several days. Technically, a draw down is defined as the cumulative loss from the last local maximum to the next local minimum (peak to trough in rough financial parlance). In many ways, by focusing on such movements, we are moving away from calendar time, and using event time instead.

A distribution of these draw downs measures how successive drops in the market can influence each other and construct a persistent process. In effect, this process measures the memory of the market. This clearly relates to many of the psychological traits outlined in Chapter 1 — especially those relating to the treatment of losses and reference points.

Johansen and Sornette find that draw downs of less than 15% are in general well captured by a distribution known as a Lévy distribution (which has fat tails). In fact the fat tail is found to decay as a power law with an index of between 0 and 2. The number of draw downs for the US market smaller than 15% is well fitted by an exponential law:

$$N(\text{DD}) = N_0 e^{-\text{DD}/\text{DC}} \quad \text{with DC} = 1.8$$

where $N(\text{DD})$ is the number of occurrences of a draw down of a given size occurring. N_0 is the total number of draw downs larger than 1% (an arbitrary cut-off level) in a century. In their fitted model, N_0 is estimated to be 2360, which is close to the full sample number of 2789. In order to be particularly fair, Johansen and Sornette use a larger estimate of DC (increasing the size of the draw downs captured by their model). In fact they use DC = 2.2. They then investigate how often large crashes are likely to be seen. Using the equation above with DC = 2.2, a crash of 28.8% or more per century is found to have probability 0.006. The return time of such an event can be found by finding the number of centuries (n) such that $0.006n \sim 1$. This yields $n \sim 160$ centuries! However, in the last century alone we have witnessed at least three such events. This clearly points to crashes being outliers rather than simply extreme events lurking in the fat tail of the distribution.

Table 5.5 Outliers

	Time period
Index	
DJIA	1900.0–2000.5
S&P500	1940.9–2000.5
Nasdaq	1971.1–2000.5
TSE300 Composite	1971.1–2000.5
All Ordinaries	1984.6–2000.5
Strait Times	1988.0–2000.5
Hang Seng	1980.1–2000.5
Nikkei 225	1973.0–2000.5
FTSE 100	1984.3–2000.5
DAX	1970.0–2000.5
MIBTel	1993.0–1999.1
Currencies	
US$/DM	1971.0–1999.4
US$/¥	1972.0–1999.4
US$/CHF	1971.0–1999.4
Commodity	
Gold	1975.0–1999.8

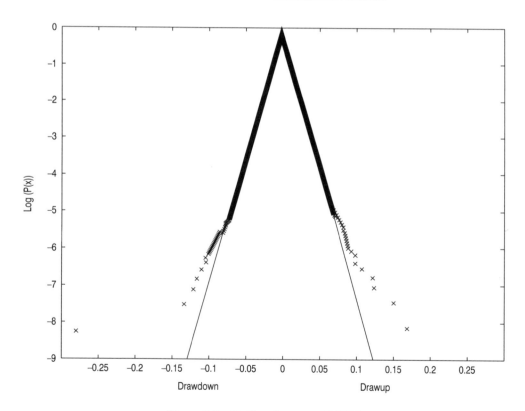

Figure 5.3 Outlier chart — S&P500

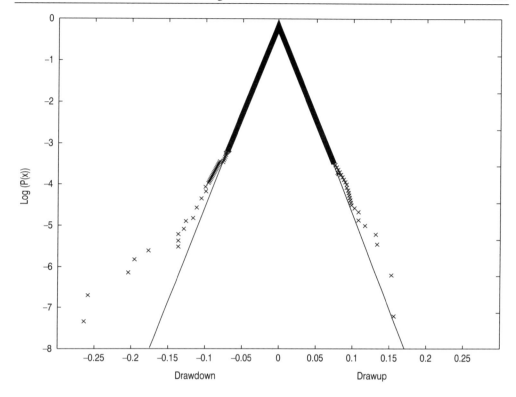

Figure 5.4   Outlier chart — NASDAQ

In order to test this finding, Johansen and Sornette create a million years of mock market data based on a GARCH model. This simulated data set is examined to see if it can generate anything like the patterns observed in the real world. It fails spectacularly to generate anywhere near enough crashes.

Nor is this evidence restricted to the US stock market. Johansen and Sornette (2001a) show that similar patterns of outliers can be found in a surprisingly wide range of markets. The DJIA, S&P500, NASDAQ, TSE300 Composite (Canada), All Ordinaries (Australia), Strait Times (Singapore), Hang Seng (Hong Kong), Nikkei 225 (Japan), FTSE 100 (UK), DAX (Germany), MIBTel (Italy), US$/DM, US$/¥, US$/CHF and gold are all found to fit the same pattern of crashes being outliers (see Table 5.5).

Figures 5.3–5.6 graphically illustrate the situation. The solid lines represent the estimated distributions with their power law decays. From a cursory glance at these charts it becomes obvious that the largest events seen in the market place are generated from an entirely different distribution, the points lie well off the solid lines of the distribution.

This suggests immediate problems for extreme value theory (EVT). This is a statistical theory much loved by the risk management industry that allows them to

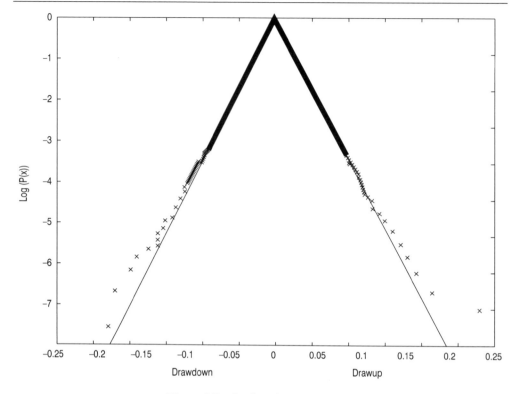

Figure 5.5 Outlier chart — Nikkei

concentrate their efforts on estimating the tail probabilities of distributions. However, EVT is not all plain sailing. Diebold, Schuermann and Stroughair (2000) point out that actually implementing EVT is exceptionally hard because the estimation procedures used are unstable within the tail probabilities.

However, from our point of view EVT has further problems. It also assumes independent returns. This implies that the degree of fatness in the tail falls as the holding length increases. Empirically, this is not the case. Returns exhibit strong correlation at the special times precisely characterized by the occurrence of extreme events. Draw downs clearly show that returns are far from independent during crisis periods.

Both crashes and more normal fat tails are the result of an endogenous self-organizing process (more on this in the next chapter), but they are not the same phenomenon. There is co-existence between self-organization and criticality. Self-organization refers to the globally stationary state of the market during normal times with fat tails. Criticality refers to the special times when crises occur. We will show in the next chapter that these periods are characterized by some rather special features, leaving clear footprints in the sand for the watching asset allocator to spot.

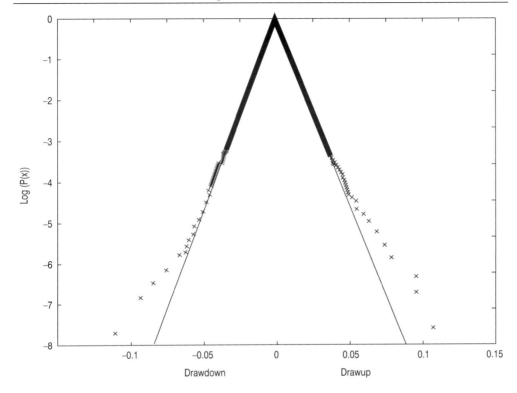

Figure 5.6   Outlier chart — $/DM

6

Asset Allocation

We might define an efficient market as one in which price is within a factor of 2 of value, i.e. price is more than half of value and less than twice value ... By this definition, I think almost all markets are efficient almost all of the time. 'Almost all' means at least 90%.

Fisher Black

6.1 INTRODUCTION

As we showed in Chapter 4, fundamentals and market prices can part company for long periods of time, even in the cleanest experimental model markets. Those results are no less relevant at the market level than they are at the stock level. However, tactical asset allocation (TAA) has had a rough ride over the 1990s, largely as a result of the performance-damaging decision by many TAAers to underweight equities for most of the decade. Given this historical record it is tempting to agree with Black's quotation above, that markets are largely efficient.

However, we think that Black's factor of 2 gives room for performance enhancement via TAA. That is we are in a sorry state if we can't choose between stocks and bonds unless they are massively out of line with each other. This chapter aims to explore mechanisms for divining the relative valuation of equities vs. bonds.

6.2 MARKETS AND FUNDAMENTALS

To illustrate that the findings of the experimental markets are valid at the market level, we will examine a simple model of the fundamentals of the S&P500. In 1981, Robert Shiller wrote a seminal paper examining potential excess volatility. That is to say, whether stock markets move more than the underlying dividend process. In order to calculate fundamental value, Shiller used a dividend discount model. He combined this with the assumption of perfect foresight. That simply means that investors forecast exactly what dividends will actually be — ultra rationality if you like:

$$P_t^* = \sum_{i=t+1}^{\infty} \frac{D_i}{(1+r)^i}$$

with P^* being the fundamental value, D_i being the dividend at time i and r being the discount rate.

Shiller conducted the analysis in real (inflation-adjusted) terms, and used the long-term real average return on equities (7.4% between 1987 and 2000) as the discount rate. Of course, as the equation above shows we would need to integrate to infinity in order to solve this problem — clearly an impossible task. However, a clever trick results from the use of the perfect foresight assumption, allowing us to calculate the outcome by guessing the solution and working backwards.

Effectively, the fundamental process from this dividend discount model is a very long run moving average of the dividends. The sensitivity of the resulting fundamental process to the guess of the end data point is shown in Figure 6.1. As can clearly be seen, differences from the end point faded relatively rapidly, such that by 1980 there is no difference in the fundamental series regardless of the chosen endpoint. It also makes it clear that the latest observations are the most dependent upon the end point selected.

Figure 6.2 shows the picture when Shiller first published his findings in 1981. It certainly shows the excessively volatile nature of the market relative to the underlying fundamentals. It also clearly shows that the market can remain dislocated from fundamentals for very extended periods of time. Twenty year dislocations are not uncommon over this sample.

The updated chart (Figure 6.3) is even more frightening. The post-1994 situation is brought starkly home. The US market has exploded in real terms, but our measure of the fundamental value has failed to keep track. As uncomfortable as the slide of 2000/2001 has been for investors, it doesn't even come close to redressing the gap between prices and values.

It should be noted that this doesn't mean that a stock market crash of catastrophic proportions is imminent. As we will show below, such a high market may imply that investors are simply expecting some very low returns for a prolonged period of time.

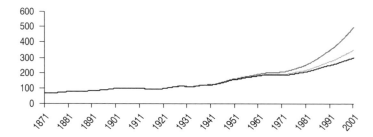

Figure 6.1   The choice of end point selection on the fundamental process

Figure 6.2   Excess volatility: 1871–1981

Source: Shiller (1981). Reproduced with permission
from the American Economic Association.

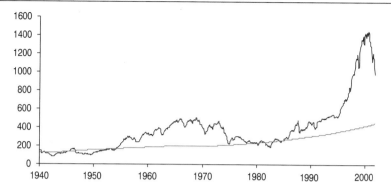

Figure 6.3 Shiller updated 1940–2001

Source: Shiller data.

6.3   DIVIDEND YIELD, SPREADS AND RATIOS

The dividend yield (D/P) was one of the first indicators used for tactical asset allocation or market timing as it was previously called. It was usually compared against some measure of the risk-free rate. This resultant spread was a crude measure of the equity risk premium. In actual fact, in order to place this interpretation on the spread, we need to assume that the long-term growth rate of dividends is constant (Figure 6.4).

Figure 6.5 shows the very long history of the dividend yield for the US market. A cursory glance at the chart reveals several significant features. Firstly, the dividend yield is at its lowest level ever. The supporters of 'New Era' thinking are quick to point out that the collapse in the dividend yield implies it is no longer a good guide to market valuations. It is missing something — namely repurchases (see Figure 6.6).

It is undeniably true that corporate financial policy has undergone a major shift over the 1990s. Repurchases have gained favour as a tax-efficient method of redistributing

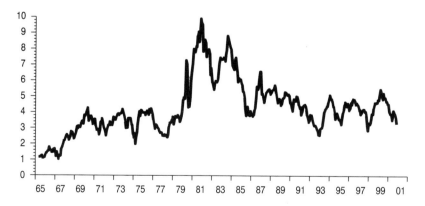

Figure 6.4 Dividend yield spread

Data Source: Thomson Datastream.

Figure 6.5   Long run dividend yield ratio
Data Source: Thomson Datastream.

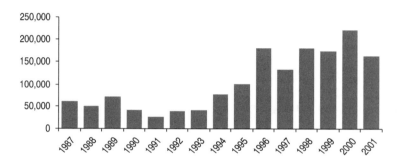

Figure 6.6   Repurchases (US$m)

cash to share holders. For firms in the S&P500, buybacks have grown from 10% of dividends in 1980 to surpassing dividends in 1997/8! Several studies have attempted to adjust the dividend yield in order to account for the rise in importance of repurchases. When some of a firm's dividends are replaced by share repurchases, the result is a reduction in shares outstanding and an associated boost to *per share* earnings and dividend growth. However, many firms that repurchase stock also issue equity, primarily to satisfy employee exercises of stock options.

Thus some adjustment needs to be made for this issuance. Liang and Sharpe (1999) is the definitive work in this field. They find repurchases have reduced shares outstanding for the largest members of the S&P500 by around 2% p.a. However, owing to the exercise of employee stock options, only around half of these shares were actually retired. Hence, Liang and Sharpe suggest that to account for repurchases, the dividend yield needs to be adjusted upwards by around 1% in the late 1990s. However, they conclude 'Over the long haul, assuming corporations need to retain 40 to 50% of their earnings to invest and grow at historical rates, the cash outflow from repurchases (net proceeds from stock option exercises) could fall back to less than half its current level. If so, the long run average pace of net share retirements would fall to only $\frac{1}{4}$ to $\frac{1}{2}$ percent

per annum'. These findings are confirmed by Montier (2002b). I find that the vast
majority of share repurchases are offset by equity issuance relating to option plans.
Figures 6.7 and 6.8 show the difference between the various measures of buybacks, and
their impact upon the yield return to investors. Even making these adjustments it
becomes clear that the dividend yield is still at the very bottom of its long-run range.

The second feature that Figure 6.5 illustrates is that the ratio itself is highly
persistent. That is to say it changes only very slowly over time. It seems almost

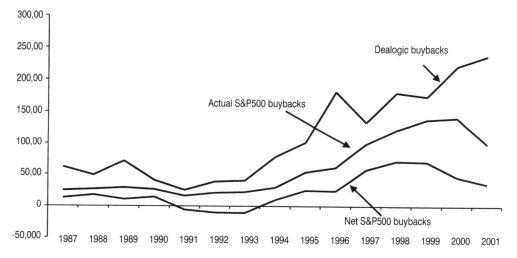

Figure 6.7   When is a buyback not a buyback?
Source: DKWR.

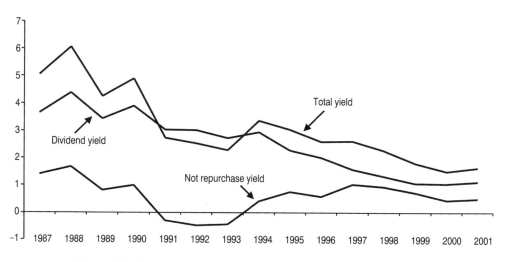

Figure 6.8   Repurchases and their impact: total yield on the S&P500
Source: DKWR.

incredulous that the dividend yield could ever have been used as a tool for tactical asset allocation, it seems better suited to use in strategic asset allocation.

Fisher and Statman (2000) explore some of the psychological errors that are made in the TAA process. In particular, they show that confirmation bias is prevalent. Confirmation bias refers to a situation where people tend to overweight information that agrees with their views, and ignore information that challenges their personal opinion.

People only remember that the dividend yield was low when the market generated a low return (i.e. crashed). To overcome this bias, the easiest thing to do is to construct a table such as Table 6.1. It shows the number of years in which a low dividend yield was followed by a low return (33 years), and the number of years in which it was followed by a high return (31 years).

Alternatively, a cross plot of the dividend yield and one year returns provides a similar picture, for those who prefer graphics to numerics. A regression line with a very flat gradient is the graphical equivalent to the table analysis. Either way, it becomes immediately transparent that virtually no short-term relationship exists between dividend yields and returns (Figure 6.9).

However, just because the dividend yield doesn't forecast short-term returns doesn't mean that we can ignore the message it sends. The dividend yield is highly persistent,

Table 6.1 Relationship between dividend yield and one year equity returns (1872–1999, US)

	Below median return	Above median return	Total
Below median D/P	33	31	64
Above median D/P	31	33	64
Total	**64**	**64**	**128**

Source: Fisher and Statman (2000).

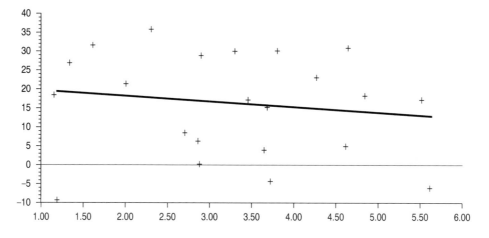

Figure 6.9 Dividend yield and one year stock returns

Data Source: Thomson Datastream.

Table 6.2   Variance decomposition of dividend yield (%)

	Dividend growth	Expected returns
Real	−34	138
Nominal	30	85

but not totally so. It does tend to cross the mean value about once a decade. High dividend yields in the 1950s preceded the high returns of the 1960s. The low dividend yield of the 1960s preceded the poor returns of the 1970s. High dividend yields in the 1970s preceded the boom of the late 1980s/1990s.

A low dividend yield must mean that either dividends are expected to grow faster than they have done in the past, or that returns will be lower than they have been in the past. Unfortunately, statistical analysis shows that low dividend yields actually generally forecast low returns not higher dividend growth rates.

Table 6.2 shows how much of the variation in the dividend yield is accounted for by changing expectations about dividend growth, and how much is accounted for by changes in expected returns. When examined in real terms, real dividend growth and the dividend yield are negatively related, such that all the variation in the dividend yield comes from expected returns.

Incidentally, Vuolteenaho (2000) carries out a similar analysis based on the price to book ratio rather than the dividend yield. His results are very similar at the aggregate level, the vast majority of variations in price to book are driven by changing expectations about returns, whilst only a small minority come from growth factors.

Given that the dividend yield is mean-reverting, albeit slowly, its implications can't be ignored. Cochrane (2001) suggests an analogy with the weather. Think of it this way, if it is −10° in London in February, the best forecast is that over the next four months or so the temperature will rise 0.5° per day. The temperature may rise or fall 20° in a few days — effectively we can explain little of the day-to-day variation, However, it is still the best forecast to say that by the late Spring/early Summer, the temperature will be significantly higher.

Translating this into the current discussion, a low dividend yield generally indicates that future returns will be low. However, this in turn begs the question, how well adjusted are investors to the prospect of low long-run returns from equities? We will turn to this question in Section 6.6.

6.4   EARNINGS YIELD, SPREADS AND RATIOS

The earnings yield of a stock market is of course the inverse of the PE, but translating this into yield terms makes comparisons with bonds far easier. See Tables 6.3 and 6.4. The standalone earnings yield is about as useful as the standalone dividend yield.

However, it is usually the ratio or spread between the earnings yield and the bond yield that is examined. The earnings yield–bond yield spread (or ratio) has little foundation in theory. However, pragmatism and practicality have made it a perennial favourite amongst practitioners such as ourselves. It certainly avoids the repurchase issue that plagues the dividend model. Earnings yields may have one slight advantage over dividend

Table 6.3 One year returns following the six lowest earnings yields (%)

Year	Earning yields at beginning of the year	Stock return during the year
1999	3.11	21.03
1995	3.76	4.92
1992	3.82	7.67
1922	3.88	27.65
1998	4.12	28.58
1934	4.17	−1.44

Table 6.4 Lowest one year returns and earnings yields (%)

Year	Earnings yield at the start of the year	Stock return during the year
1931	6.06	−43.4
1937	5.81	−35.03
1974	8.47	−26.47
1930	7.41	−24.90
1877	7.87	−16.88
1973	5.43	−14.66

yields. A stock's dividend yield (like a bond's current yield) represents the periodic cash return to the investor. However, stock holders also benefit from that part of earnings that is retained, via an increase in the book value of the business. When considering bonds, the underlying principal value is constant, whereas with equities (it is hoped) the underlying book value grows over time. Earnings yields can thus be thought of as a total theoretical return. Over time, however, earnings yields are likely to understate a stock's appreciation, since stocks tend to sell at some multiple of book value.

An alternative way of looking at the situation is to say that earnings yields contain two elements, a dividend yield and a retained earnings yield. If investment by corporates is efficient then the future dividend growth should be higher than or equal to the retained earnings growth. Otherwise, investors would have been better having the cash back in the first place.

If, on the other hand, investment is inefficient then future growth will be below the retained earnings yield. Table 6.5 shows the decomposition of the earnings yield into the dividend yield and the retained earnings yield. We have also shown the growth in real dividends achieved over the subsequent 10 years.

The results don't make comfortable reading for those who believe that corporate managers know best. In general, corporate managers have consistently failed to deliver real dividend growth even close to the retained earnings yield.

One of the biggest flaws of this model is of course the fact that it depends upon earnings. As we have noted several times elsewhere in this book, earnings are the construct of accountants, and shifts in the reporting basis of earnings can wreak havoc on measures such as earnings yields.

Table 6.5 Efficient investment — sadly not

Decade	Earnings yield (%)	Dividend yield (%)	Retained earnings yield (%)	Delivered real dividend growth rate (%)
1950–60	13.8	6.8	7.0	2.6
1960–70	5.8	3.2	2.6	2.8
1970–80	6.3	3.5	2.8	−1.3
1980–90	13.5	5.1	8.4	1.8
1990–00	6.6	4.2*	2.4	1.3

*Adjusted for net repurchases.
Source: DKWR.

There are two main variants of earnings yield spreads or ratios. One uses the historical PE (trailing), the other uses a forward-looking PE (consensus). We have found that the prospective bond equity earnings ratio (PBEER) performs the best when put under the strain of the real world. It uses the earnings yield derived from the I/B/E/S consensus earnings estimates, and compares it against the current nominal bond yield (Figure 6.10).

One of the key reasons that we prefer this measure is that it captures the market consensus for earnings growth, at least for the next 12 months. So we capture at least an element of market sentiment and dynamics. Indeed so popular is this particular model that it has even found its way into speeches by Federal Reserve Chairman, Alan Greenspan! Lander, Orpanides and Douvogiannis (1997) show it is possible to trade the S&P500 profitably on the basis on this indicator.

A key question that must be answered by users is the reference point to which the current level of the PBEER is to be compared. Our own investigations suggest that a recent sample average is perhaps the best measure. As we have noted elsewhere, the

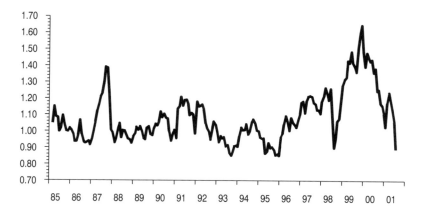

Figure 6.10 Prospective bond equity earnings ratio
Data Source: Thomson Datastream.

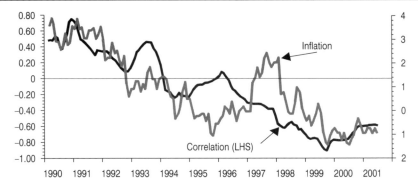

Figure 6.11 Correlation between bonds and equities — the Japanese example

Data Source: Thomson Datastream.

equity risk premium is clearly not constant over long samples. Yet a model such as
PBEER is implicitly assuming a constant ERP. Therefore to minimize the risk of being
confused by shifts in the ERP, a five year moving average is probably the best measure
of the 'equilibrium' level of the PBEER.

An alternative is to consider outside events that might cause a shift in the correlation
between bonds and equities. As we have already noted, limited arbitrage implies that
correlations can and do shift over time for market and fundamental reasons. For
instance, *a priori* it could be expected that the inflation environment may affect both
bonds and equities. As Figure 6.11 shows, the relationship between inflation and the
rolling 36 month correlation between Japanese bonds and equities seems clear.
Deflation is great news for bonds, but a disaster for firms who find themselves long real
assets and short nominal ones. The result is to drive the correlation between bonds and
stocks from positive to negative.

It should also be noted that during times of sheer market panic, the bond yield is
usually dropped in favour of a cash yield, and frequently the prospective earnings yield
is replaced with its historical equivalent on the grounds that during panics no one trusts
analysts' earning estimates. So when looking for market bottoms following crashes,
watch the earnings cash yield. This serves as an important lesson in pragmatism for the
practitioner. It isn't worth getting wed to one indicator. If other market participants are
using an indicator, it is as well to use it too, if only because it serves as a guide to their
likely flow dynamics and, as we saw in the style life cycle model, these flows have major
market impacts.

6.5 PAYOUT RATIO

Unlike the previous two indicators, which are widely used by practitioners, the idea of
using the payout ratio may seem slightly odd. However, Lamont (1998) shows that it
can be a very useful indicator. He finds that high dividends forecast high returns, but
that high earnings forecast low returns. Earnings are clearly closely correlated with
business cycle conditions, and it is this correlation that gives them predictive powers
over stock returns. Risk premia on stocks co-vary negatively with current economic

activity. Investors require higher expected returns during recessions, and lower expected returns during booms. Since earnings vary with economic activity, current earnings predict future returns. In contrast, dividends are essentially permanent. Once a firm has raised its dividend it is exceptionally unlikely to cut it again (in a hurry). As such, high dividends suggest a high return going forward. See Figures 6.12 and 6.13.

Interestingly, Lamont finds that the payout ratio has relatively high predictive powers for short-run returns. However, for forecasting long-run returns, any relatively smooth accounting variable seems to provide very similar pictures, i.e. earnings, dividends or any series that captures nominal growth produces a long-run forecast of very low returns for the US market currently.

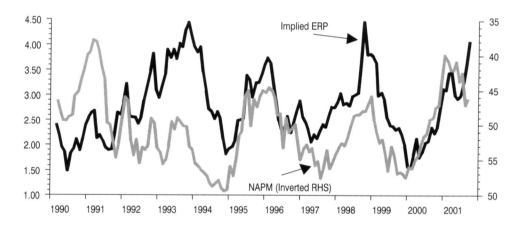

Figure 6.12   Implied ERP and the NAPM

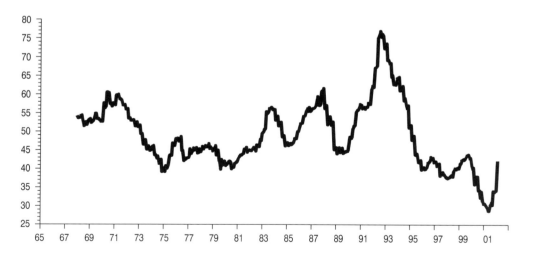

Figure 6.13   Payout ratio

Data Source: Thomson Datastream.

6.6   THE EQUITY RISK PREMIUM

All the above measures really serve as a proxy for the equity risk premium, which of course begs the question, why not look directly at what we are actually interested in? Several times already in this book we have used an implied equity risk premium, so it should come as no surprise to readers that we feel this is one of the best ways of conducting asset allocation work.

Of course, in order to estimate the implied equity premium we need a model of the process underlying stock prices. As noted before, our own preference is for a very simple approach. Our measure of the implied equity premium is:

Implied equity premium = Current dividend yield + Long-term growth − Bond yield

This of course raises questions over the assumption on long-term growth. Should we use the 3–5 year forecast from consensus analysts adjusted for the payout ratio, or the long-term nominal growth rate of the economy? As noted in Chapter 1, we tend to use both to provide a check against each other. Figure 6.14 shows the top-down (long-term nominal growth rate) and the bottom-up (payout ratio × long-term earnings expectations) implied equity risk premia.

One of the features that immediately stands out from a chart of our implied equity risk premium is just how cyclical it is. This makes sense in terms of the framework we mentioned in Chapter 1 on dynamic prospect theory. People's attitudes towards risk change dependent upon their past experiences. If the stock market has gone up a lot from the point at which the investor bought in (her reference point) then the market is perceived as being less risky, hence the drop in the implied equity risk premium.

Barberis, Huang and Santos (2000) examine a model where investors have these kinds of preferences, i.e. they are loss-averse in general (disliking losses more than liking gains of equal size) and have a perception of risk governed by past investment performance. They find that this generates a time-varying risk premium, which in turn

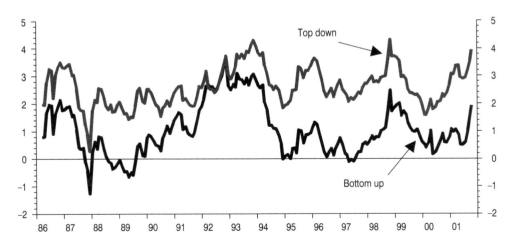

Figure 6.14   Implied equity risk premium
Data Source: Thomson Datastream.

causes prices to be much more volatile than underlying dividends (just as we saw in the
Shiller model of the S&P500). When this excess volatility is combined with investors'
innate loss aversion, the model generates a large equity risk premium, just as we observe
in the real data.

Claus and Thomas (2000) use what they term an abnormal earnings model to derive
an implied equity risk premium. Abnormal earnings valuation is just another term for
the residual income approach, or EVA if you prefer. The approach recognizes that
dividends equal earnings less changes in accounting (or book) values of equity, and
allows the stream of projected dividends to be replaced by the current book value of
equity plus a function of future accounting earnings. Although it is isomorphic to the
dividend present value model, the abnormal earnings approach uses other information
that is currently available to reduce the importance of assumed growth rates, and
narrows the range of allowable growth rates by focusing on growth in rents, rather than
dividend growth.

Figure 6.15 shows the time series of the implied ERP for the US market using the
Claus and Thomas methodology. Their estimates are considerably less volatile than our
simple model. This is to be expected because they are modelling more features than are
captured by our simple little model.

Claus and Thomas (2000) also examine the implied equity risk premium for a number
of international markets. The results observed for Japan are perhaps the most
interesting. They suggest that the equity premium in Japan increased during the sample
period, from about −1% in the early 1990s to 2% in the late 1990s. These results are
also consistent with a stock market bubble that has gradually burst. That is, early in the
sample period prices were systematically higher than the fundamentals (represented by
analysts' forecasts) would suggest, and they have gradually declined to a level that is
supported by analysts' forecasts (Table 6.6).

In a recent survey of financial economists, Welch (1999) found that on average the
equity risk premium was expected to be around 6–7%. Such a high number suggested
that finance academics are anchored on the historical average performance of equities.
However, in an update to the survey Welch (2001) found that the 10 year equity risk
premium expected by academic finance specialists has fallen to 5%. The 2001 Welch
survey also highlighted the importance of the time horizon in any discussion of the

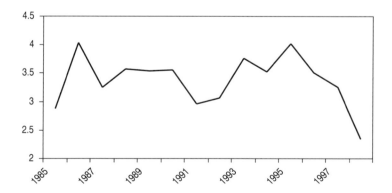

Figure 6.15 Claus and Thomas ERP measure

Table 6.6   Estimates of the implied ERP

Year	France	Germany	Japan	UK
1987	2.06			
1988	4.00	3.43		
1989	3.64	3.87		3.17
1990	3.04	1.10		2.57
1991	2.94	1.03	−0.95	2.47
1992	2.26	2.16	−0.86	2.77
1993	2.31	0.70	−1.05	3.29
1994	1.70	1.30	−1.04	2.87
1995	2.06	2.22	1.12	3.02
1996	2.38	2.14	0.79	3.34
1997	2.28	2.28	1.65	2.53
1998	2.53		1.99	2.09

Reproduced from Claus and Thomas, 'Equity premia as low as 3%', Journal of Finance (2000), with permission from Blackwell Publishers.

ERP. When asked for their expectation of the one year ERP, the academics had an average forecast of 3%. It is interesting to note that 30 out of the 510 surveyed actually had a negative equity risk premium expectation over a one year time horizon. Vuolteenaho (2000) shows that his price to book model suggests an equity risk premium of 1–3% going forward. At a recent conference I attended, fund managers were surveyed and settled on an equity risk premium of 5%.

Graham and Harvey (2001) offer a very different view on the equity risk premium by surveying Chief Financial Officers (CFOs). The key results from the study are shown in Figure 6.16. The CFOs were asked to provide estimates on the expected equity risk premium over two time horizons — one year and 30 years. The one year expected ERP is, unsurprisingly, highly volatile. However, the 30 year expected equity risk premium is much more stable, and around 4%.

The real total return that an investor receives can be broken down into three components: dividend yield, real dividend growth and multiple expansion. Figure 6.17 shows the decomposition for long-run returns, juxtaposed with the last five years' experience. In the long run, the dividend yield component has accounted for some 52% of the real average return that investors have received. In marked contrast, over the last five years, investors' real returns have been dominated by multiple expansion, which has accounted for no less than 80% of their total real return. Our fear is that too many investors are anchoring on the experience of the immediate past in forming their long-run equity return expectations.

Of course, this multiple expansion would be perfectly justified if future growth was to offset it. However, as Campbell and Shiller (1988) show this have never been the case before, and there is no reason to believe that this time is different. Using the same decomposition introduced above, we can form an expectation about the total return that investors are likely to receive in the future.

For starters, investors will receive the current dividend yield of 1.7%. Then comes the contentious issue of long-term real dividend growth. Real dividend growth can't exceed real economic growth in the very long run. Moreover, a substantial element

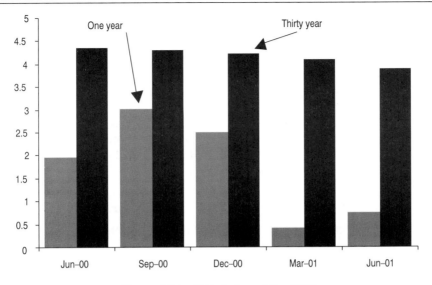

Figure 6.16   CFOs' view of the ERP

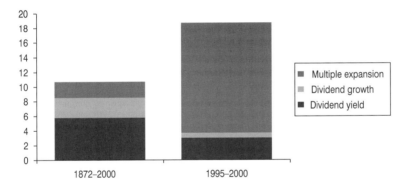

Figure 6.17   Decomposition of returns

of economic growth is provided by new firms that are not in existence (let alone
investable). Hence real dividend growth is effectively capped below the rate of growth in
the whole economy. To be as charitable as possible, we have included a 3% real
dividend growth rate. This is roughly equivalent to saying that the real economy could
grow at 5%, with no more than 40% of that growth generated by new firms.

We have assumed no multiple expansion. We feel it would be dangerous to
extrapolate the historical contribution that multiple expansion has made. After all, to
generate the same 2.2% p.a. return attributable to multiple expansion between 1872
and 2001 would require the dividend yield to fall to 0.3% over the next 100 years or so.
We need to adjust the total return to acknowledge the role of repurchases as outlined
above.

However, even after making this adjustment, it implies that the US market is implying a total real return of just over 5% p.a. over the long term! (Composed of 1.7% dividend yield, a 0.5% adjustment for repurchases over the long run, and a 3% real dividend growth rate.) This doesn't seem much of a compensation for risk to us. In fact, taking the current yield on Treasury Inflation Protected securities of 3–3.5% implies the market is expecting a real equity risk premium of just 1.5%!

This doesn't sit well with the actual expectations unearthed above. Even the most conservative of the survey measures suggested an equity risk premium of 4%, more than double the market implied long-run equity risk premium! Either prices need to fall to restore future returns, or investors will have to get used to being seriously disappointed by the long-run returns to stocks.

6.7   SHOULD CORPORATE FINANCIERS BE RUNNING TAA?

The title of this section probably has you panicking already. But don't worry, we don't really mean that corporate financiers should deign to come out from their rarified offices and get their hands dirty in the secondary markets. Rather that much of the information created by the activities of corporate financiers may actually be useful in the tactical asset allocation process.

6.7.1   IPOs and SEOs

There is a mass of evidence that firms effectively time the equity market with their issuance. That is to say that firms conducting initial public offerings (IPOs) or seasoned equity offerings (SEOs) underperform the broader market.

So why not use information contained in equity issuance as a guide to market timing? The aggregate change in shares may predict total market returns for the same reasons that changes in shares in issue are correlated with stock returns in the cross-section. When the expected return implied by the valuations of the market are low relative to the yields on other assets (i.e. stock prices are high), corporations can access a relatively cheap source of funds by issuing shares. Conversely, when expected returns are high (i.e. stock prices are low) then firms may find shares an attractive investment (repurchases).

We will cover the potential reasons for this dramatic underperformance of equity issuers in Chapter 7. For the purposes of the current situation an awareness of the existence of such patterns will be sufficient, plus an understanding that the overwhelming evidence suggests this is caused by serious investor over-optimism.

The latest data on US IPOs shows that, like SEOs, they tend to underperform the broad market (Tables 6.7 and 6.8). However, when matched by style and size (i.e. price to book and market cap) IPOs do not tend to underperform. That is to say that they match the returns of small cap growth stocks more generally. Of course, it is worth noting that this sample necessarily excludes the dot.com bubble of the last few years — it is hard to imagine that when these stocks are eventually included in the sample any benchmark based on style will be beaten.

Not only do equity offerings underperform the broader market in general, but they appear to suffer cycles, in terms of the volume coming to market and in terms of the scale of the initial return (the difference between the closing price on the first day of

Table 6.7 Mean % returns on US SEOs (1970–1998) five years after issuing

SEO firms	10.1
Size matched	14.6
Difference	−4.6
SEO firms	10.6
Style and size matched	14.2
Difference	−3.6

Source: Reprinted from 'Investment banking and securities issuance', J. Ritter, copyright (2001), with permission of Elsevier Science.

Table 6.8 Mean % returns on US IPOs (1970–1998) five years after issuing

IPO firms	10.7
Size matched	14.1
Difference	−3.4
IPO firms	11.0
Style and size matched	10.8
Difference	0.2

Source: Reprinted from 'Investment banking and securities issuance', J. Ritter, copyright (2001), with permission of Elsevier Science.

trading and the offer price). IPOs in particular tend to cluster around the peak of markets (Figure 6.18).

Nelson (1999), Baker and Wurgler (2000) and Schill (2000) all investigate the hypothesis that high equity issuance is a good predictor of forthcoming poor general market conditions. All three studies use a different measure of equity issuance. Nelson uses the percentage change in the number of shares outstanding (excluding mergers). Baker and Wurgler focus on gross equity issuance as a percentage of total equity and debt issuance. Schill uses the volume of IPOs as a percentage of total listed firms as his measure.

One word of caution to practitioners: don't be tempted to use the Federal Reserve's flow of funds data on equity issuance for the purpose of timing the market. As people familiar with the data will know, this series shows that over the 1990s firms have had a massive negative net issuance. However, the flow of funds data are dominated by exchange issues and retirements associated with merger and acquisition activity. Merger activity is generally significantly larger than normal financing operations and considerably more volatile. As we will see in the next chapter, merger activity may be driven by very different motives than the normal financing decisions of selling or buying equity.

Figure 6.19 is taken from Baker and Wurgler's study. It shows the mean value-weighted return on the US market by equity issuance in the prior year. As becomes immediately clear from the chart, when equity issuance as a percentage of total equity and debt issuance is in the highest quartile, then on average the US market has delivered a negative return of around 10%. Conversely, when equity issuance is rare

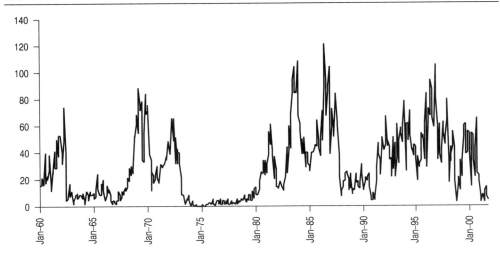

Figure 6.18 IPO volume

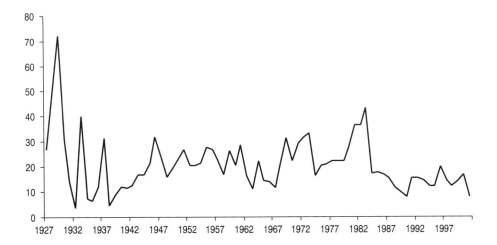

Figure 6.19 The equity share of new issues

Source: Baker and Wurgler (2000). Reproduced
from Blackwell Publishers.

(quartile 1) then the mean return on the US market is high, at over 25%. Baker and
Wurgler also find that equity issuance is a better indicator of market returns than many
of the usual suspects such as dividend yield and even price to book (Figure 6.20).

Nor are these results limited purely to the US market. We have found similar patterns
in our UK data (albeit a much smaller sample size). Figure 6.21 documents a surge
in IPOs during the run up to the bursting of the Japanese stock market bubble of the
late 1980s/early 1990s. So the international evidence on the usefulness of IPO data is
building.

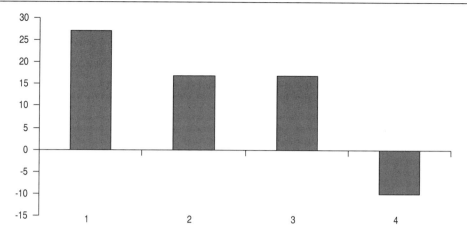

Figure 6.20   Market returns as a function of equity issuance (1927–1997)

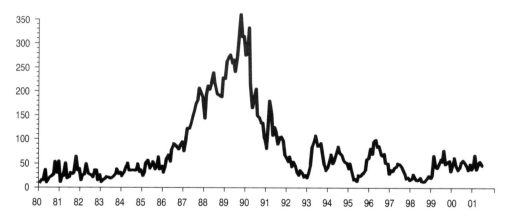

Figure 6.21   Japan equity issuance
Data Source: Thomson Datastream.

6.7.2 Acquisition Financing

Like IPOs, mergers and acquisitions tend to cycle. Mergers tend to be relatively clustered in time, and focused in periods of high stock market valuation. The exception to this general rule is the 1980s, when valuations were relatively low, but acquisitions were high. Interestingly, Andrade, Mitchell and Stafford (2001) report that all-cash transactions accounted for 45.6% of total mergers during 1980–1989. This compares with only 27.4% being all cash-financed during 1990–1998.

This suggests another indicator that might prove useful in TAA decisions. The empirical evidence suggests that stock-financed mergers tend to suffer considerably worse negative excess returns than cash-financed mergers. In addition, growth stocks involved in mergers and acquisitions tend to suffer higher negative excess returns than value stocks. Once again, this will be investigated in more depth in the next chapter, but for now, accept that growth stocks tend to use equity as currency in mergers and acquisitions more than value stocks (Figure 6.22).

So in general, firms conduct transactions using stock as payment when it is cheap currency (i.e. overvalued), and use cash when stock is expensive (undervalued). Hence the ratio of stock-financed to cash-financed deals should contain information as to the valuation of the market. Our initial investigations into this area suggest that this indicator could again be very useful. Figure 6.23 shows the ratio of stock-financed to cash-financed deals in the US market. The rule seems clear, buy when the ratio dips below 0.6, and sell when the ratio exceeds 1.

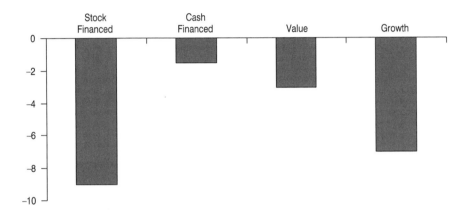

Figure 6.22   Stock/non-stock, growth vs. value

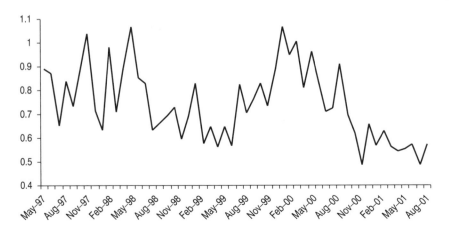

Figure 6.23   Stock vs. cash financing

6.7.3   Insider Trading

The key problem for testing the usefulness of insider trading as a guide to the level of valuations is working out what the insider's time horizons are. If they are acting before a period of positive abnormal returns, purchases above normal carry a high probability of detection, however, a lower level of sales by insiders compared with normal carries a much reduced risk of detection.

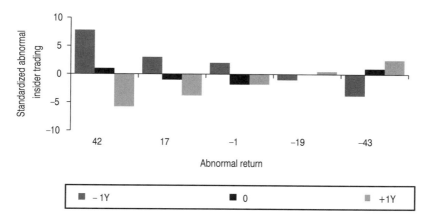

Figure 6.24   Insider buys minus insider sales in years around abnormal performance

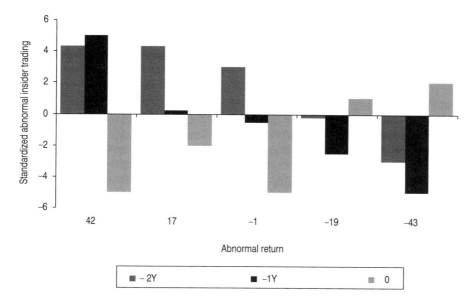

Figure 6.25   Longer lead window

Conversely, if insiders are acting ahead of negative abnormal returns, sales above their normal level would carry a high risk of detection, whereas purchases below their normal level would be unlikely to be spotted. Petitt (2000)[1] examines some 100,000 open market insider trades between 1980 and 1990 for all stocks listed on the NYSE/AMEX firms. Two thirds of the number of trades are sales, representing 80% of the total value of trades.

In order to assess the impact of insider trades we need to identify a time horizon. Petitt took the year before the abnormal return, the year of the abnormal return, and the year after the abnormal return. Figure 6.24 shows the result of the study. In the year prior to a very high abnormal return insiders are significant buyers, during the year itself insiders don't do very much, and then following the abnormal return they turn into net sellers.

Conversely, in the run up to negative abnormal returns insiders are noticeably significant sellers. Once again this appears to be largely unwound during the year after the poor stock performance. Widening the event window to cover the two years before the abnormal return shows that insiders anticipate abnormal returns well in advance, with the trends outlined above also being evident in the two year run up event window (Figure 6.25).

Lakonishok and Lee (2001) also show that insider trades can contain useful signals about future market movements. They study all firms listed on the NYSE, AMEX and NASDAQ between 1975 and 1995. In general they find evidence to support the idea that insiders time the market relatively effectively, and are contrarian in their approach. However, they also note that this result is concentrated in the smaller end of the market. See Figures 6.26 and 6.27.

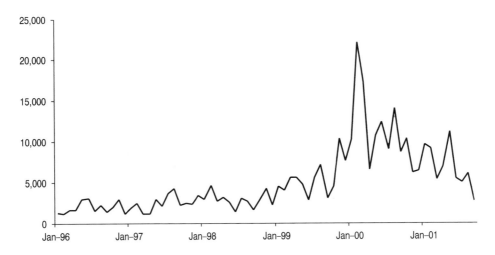

Figure 6.26   Insider sales (US$m)

[1] Unpublished notes.

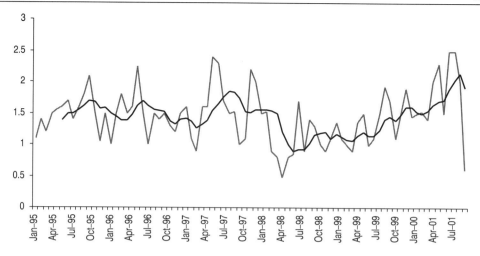

Figure 6.27   Insider sell/buy ratio

6.8   MARKET LIQUIDITY

As we documented in Chapter 4, liquidity has a role in asset pricing models (and hence in explaining the cross-section results). However, there is also a strong case to say that liquidity is important in time series results as well (Jones, 2000).

Baker and Stein (2001) build a model to explain the role of liquidity in the time series results. The intuition behind their model is easy to understand. First, there is a class of irrational investors who under-react to the information contained in order flows. The presence of these agents lowers the price impact of any trade, and hence boosts liquidity. The second key element of their model is that short sale constraints exist. The short sale constraints imply that irrational investors will only be active in the market when their valuations are higher than those of the rational investors. That is when sentiment is positive and as a result the market is overvalued.

When the sentiment of the irrational investors is negative, the short sale constraints keep them out of the market. Since the irrational investors tend to make the market more liquid, measures of liquidity provide an indicator of the relative presence or absence of these investors, and hence the level of prices relative to fundamentals.

Baker and Stein go on to test the proposition that turnover can serve as a proxy for market liquidity, and hence the presence of irrational investors. They construct an annual turnover series by taking the ratio of reported NYSE volume to average shares listed (alternatives include the average return to the average volume — a rough measure of price impact). They de-trend this series using a five year moving average. Baker and Stein show that such an indicator has explanatory power both in univariate tests and multivariate tests as well. In their univariate test, Baker and Stein show that a one standard deviation rise in their measure (equivalent to turnover going from the 1932 level to the 1998 level, 30 to 42%) reduces expected returns by roughly 13%! (See Figure 6.28.)

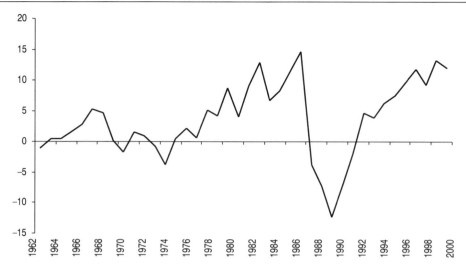

Figure 6.28   Turnover as a sentiment indicator

6.9   CRASHES AS CRITICAL POINTS

One of the over-riding lessons of this book is that we shouldn't be afraid to peek outside our own narrow field of specialization and into findings from other disciplines. The basic premise of this work is that we can learn more about the way in which financial markets function by studying insights from the field of psychology. We have also used biological models to explore the survival of irrationality in markets, and the life cycle of investment styles. In terms of timing markets, the greatest insights seem to be offered by physicists.

There is a long tradition of idea swapping amongst the physical sciences. Indeed some of the most exciting developments in recent times have come from interdisciplinary studies in complexity. In the softer sciences, this interdisciplinary cross-fertilization is somewhat harder to come by. However, physicists have recently started to become increasingly interested in financial markets. The particular field in which the recent developments have been made goes by the uninspiring name of statistical mechanics.

Statistical mechanics covers a wide range of subjects from thermodynamics to material fatigue. It is relevant to the analysis of financial markets because it deals with describing complex behaviour in systems in terms of their simple basic constituents, and simple interaction laws. Complexity arises from interaction of the basic constituents in terms of co-operation and competition. Complexity is often said to exist on the edge of chaos. The implications of chaos theory for investment have been explored in depth by Peters (1998, 1999). However, complexity is still a relatively youthful area of study. It deals with situations that are neither perfectly ordered nor chaotic. Instead complexity reflects influences of both these structures.

Much of the work on complexity has been carried out at the Santa Fe Institute (SFI). Chris Langton of the SFI describes complexity as 'From the interaction of the individual components ... emerges some kind of global property ... something you couldn't have predicted from what you know of the component parts. And the global property, this emergent behaviour, feeds back to influence the behaviour of the individuals ... that produced it'. See Figure 6.29.

If the reader is anything like the author, then the parallels of Langton's description to the stock market are startling. It is to tools for analysing complex adaptive systems that we now turn our attention.

6.9.1 Crashes as Outliers

One of the most important contributions that physicists have made is analysing the distribution of returns. For a much fuller discussion of these issues see the previous chapter. It is well known that distributions of stock returns have 'fat tails' (or are leptokurtic, if you prefer the statistical jargon). That is a 5% daily loss in the DJIA occurs approximately once every two years, whereas according to the normal distribution (Gaussian) such a loss would be predicted once every 1000 years!

Johansen and Sornette (1999) point out that crashes can be seen in one of two ways:

1. The distribution of returns is stationary and extreme events can be extrapolated as lying in its far (fat) tail. This approach forms the basis of extreme value theory now being introduced into risk management.
2. Crashes cannot be accounted for by an extrapolation of the distribution of smaller events to the regime of extremes. Instead crashes actually belong to another regime or distribution altogether, and as such they are outliers in the data.

In order to examine these two rival explanations, it is necessary to examine draw downs. A draw down is defined as a persistent decrease in the index over consecutive days. Specifically, Johansen and Sornette ignored all upward movements of less than 1% on the DJIA. It was found that the distribution of the draw downs for the daily DJIA 1990–1993 was well approximated by an exponential distribution. Technically,

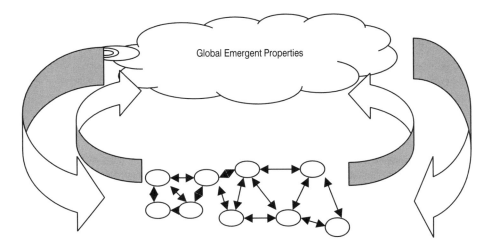

Figure 6.29 Langton's graphic view of complexity

the distribution had a decay constant of 2%. For this distribution, the chance of seeing a greater than 2% move is around 37%. However, when looking at crashes the size of 1914, 1929, 1987 an exponential distribution with a decay constant of 2% would suggest such an occurrence once about every 50 centuries, rather than three times in a single century.

In fact, for the draw down distribution a decay constant of 2% only held for draw downs of less than 15%. Moving beyond that size of draw down suggests an entirely different distribution. That is to say, crashes are outliers. This is important for our analysis because it means that we can focus on techniques that isolate crash periods, rather than worrying about the whole distribution. It is also deeply worrying from a risk management perspective, because it suggests that even advanced techniques such as extreme value theory are actually going to be too optimistic about the frequency with which we are likely to encounter crashes.

6.9.2 Critical Points in Complex Adaptive Systems

The idea that complex adaptive systems evolve towards a critical state stems from the work of Per Bak. For a very readable introduction to his ideas see Bak (1997). To describe the nature of complex adaptive systems and their march towards self-organized criticality, Bak uses the analogy of a pile of sand:

> 'Consider the scenario of a child at the beach letting sand trickle down to form a pile. In the beginning, the pile is flat, and the individual grains remain close to where they land. Their motion can be understood in terms of their physical properties. As the process continues, the pile becomes steeper, and there will be little sand slides. As time goes on, the sand slides become bigger and bigger. Eventually, some of the sand slides may even span all or most of the pile. At that point, the system is far out of balance, and its behaviour can no longer be understood in terms of the individual grains. The avalanches form a dynamic of their own, which can be understood only from a holistic description of the properties of the entire pile rather than from a reductionist description of individual grains: the sandpile is a complex system.'

Fascinating you may say, but what does this have to do with market crashes? Well we beg your indulgence for a few minutes more, but promise all will be revealed shortly. Complex adaptive systems and self-organized criticality are seen in an immense number of fields from earthquakes, solar flares and even patterns of extinction.

Even more amazing than the wide variety of examples of self-organized criticality is that they appear to all share a common foundation. The distribution of the probability of an event in each of these systems is captured well by a power law.

Power laws simply state that some quantity N can be expressed as some power of another quantity s:

$$N(s) = s^{-\tau}$$

where s could be the energy released by an earthquake, and $N(s)$ could be the number of earthquakes with that energy. We would expect to see a relatively high number of small earthquakes, and a relatively low number of really large earthquakes. We will suggest below that s could be the size of a stock market crash, and $N(s)$ could be the number of crashes of that magnitude.

When plotted in log–log space, a power law will give a straight line:

$$\log N(s) = -\tau \log s$$

The exponent of the power law is the gradient of this straight line. This representation also makes clear the important concept of scale invariance. It doesn't matter where you look on the straight line, it appears to be the same over all scales. So using this kind of analysis to spot market crashes is sometimes referred to as discrete scale invariance.

Economists need to spend far more time understanding complex adaptive systems and the power law distributions they follow. Armaral *et al.* (1996a,b) study the fluctuations in growth rates of companies of size *s*. The growth rate fluctuations are measured by the standard deviation of a variety of different measures including sales, number of employees and assets. They find that these fluctuations follow a power law $s^{-\beta}$ with $\beta \approx 0.2$. This finding suggests that firms can be modelled as complex adaptive systems; the challenge for microeconomists is to understand why this is so.

6.9.3 Financial Markets and Discrete Scale Invariance

Two of the pioneers of using discrete scale analysis in the context of stock markets are Didier Sornette and Anders Johansen. Sornette first began looking at self-organized criticality in the context of predicting the failure of pressure tanks on rockets. Sornette realized that the rupture of complex composite material structures could be understood as a complex adaptive system leading to specific detectable critical signatures.

Not only did he find power laws, but Sornette also uncovered a log-periodic pattern in the data. That is to say, as the system moved closer and closer to its critical point a sequence of oscillations with progressively shorter cycles was observed. This series of oscillations decayed according to a geometrical series.

In physics, one of the trade marks of a phase transition is increasing synchronization. A phase transition occurs when systems move between states. For instance from solid to liquid to gas (the classic example being ice, water and steam). It is this increasing synchronization that leads to the pattern of oscillations Sornette observed.

In financial markets, crashes occur because of increasing synchronization of the individual market participants. In normal market conditions, buyers and sellers are approximately equally matched, preventing massive swings in prices. However, during a crash the sellers swamp the buyers. There is an increased correlation between the actions of the market participants. Effectively, the crash is caused by a local self-reinforcing imitation between investors.

Quite why this happens remains a challenge to be explored, although recent papers by Hong and Stein (2001) and DeMarzo, Vayanos and Zwiebel (1999) have started to model the interaction amongst market participants and the way in which information is transferred amongst investors. One of the potential areas of future research involves a closer study of how memes (pronounced meems, as in teams) — which are contagious ideas — transmit themselves through markets. Lynch (1998, 2001) provides an interesting analysis of how beliefs can spread through societies and indeed financial markets. The success of any meme depends upon three critical factors: transmissivity, receptivity and longevity. Transmissivity measures how much dissemination behaviour the meme elicits from its existing hosts. A religion promising entry into the afterlife for proponents who convert others is a classic example of a meme with high transmissivity.

Receptivity refers to how believable a meme is upon first being heard. All the transmission in the world won't help spread an idea that falls upon deaf ears. To be successful a meme must sound reasonable. Longevity refers to how long a host of the meme remains a host before dropping out or dying. Think about these factors in the context of the internet bubble — transmissivity for a financial idea is high, because once you have invested the easiest way of making money is to persuade others to invest in the same stock. Receptivity was probably high because the internet as a medium was exploding, and most people could see ways in which it was impacting their daily lives. So at least two factors for meme success were certainly present during the internet bubble. It remains to be tested how far these ideas can be carried, but future research is likely to be forthcoming in this area.

As Vandewaller *et al.* (1999) demonstrate forcibly, in the context of stock markets, there is a marked tendency for volatility to cluster around stock market crashes (Figure 6.30). That is, volatility seems to increase ahead of, and directly after, a market crash ... much like the foreshocks and aftershocks associated with earthquakes. Presumably, this increase in volatility is the mirror image of increasing correlation amongst investors' trading strategies. The further away from the crash you move (in terms of time) the more balanced the market is between buyers and sellers, however, as the crash approaches so an increasing number of one-time investors become prevalent (sellers), eventually leading to the crash event itself. So we are essentially looking for a measure that quantifies the probability that a large group of agents place sell orders simultaneously, and create enough of an imbalance in the order book that market makers are unable or unwilling to absorb without altering prices dramatically.

Sornette and Johansen, and Vandewaller have pioneered the examination of financial markets for the tell-tale signs of complexity. Their search has not been in vain. Once again a pattern of power laws decorated with log-periodic oscillations of increasing cycle frequency has been unearthed. Moreover, they have found remarkable universality in their results. Approximately the same fundamental scaling ratio characterizes the log-periodic signatures. That is to say, the pattern followed by the cycles speeding up in the approach to a crash is virtually identical in the markets examined.

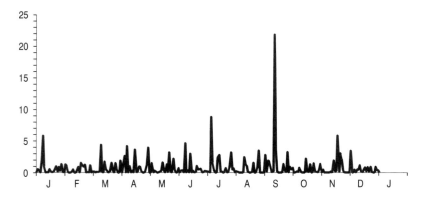

Figure 6.30   Volatility clustering in 1987
Data Source: Thomson Datastream.

Figure 6.31 was kindly provided by Vandewaller. It clearly shows the techniques we have been discussing. It examines the Dow Jones in the run up to the 1987 crash. It clearly demonstrates the accelerating power law nature of the market trend in the top half of the diagram. The lower section of the diagram beautifully shows the log-periodic oscillations we have been discussing. It is a stunning graphical display of the way in which the cycle frequency speeds up as we get closer and closer to the eventual crash.

Nor is this evidence limited to a handful of markets. Market trends best described as accelerating power laws with log-periodic oscillation have been found in a massive range of markets, as Table 6.9 illustrates. It isn't just equity markets that reveal themselves to be complex adaptive systems, foreign exchange markets also reveal the same patterns.

Interestingly, Johansen and Sornette (1999, 2001b) show that equivalent patterns emerge when the bottom of a long crash is established. That is just as the slow build-up of bullishness leads to self-organized criticality at the top of the market, so increasing capitulation is a feature of the bottom of a market. Johansen and Sornette show that the same sort of power law with log-periodic oscillations is found at the bottom of markets such as Japan in 1998, and the gold market in 1980. This symmetry of pattern in both bullish and bearish phases of the market suggests that understanding the factors or processes driving the increased long-range correlations will be a vital area of research in the near future.

This area of investigation is still embryonic. However, we think that its insights into the behaviour of financial markets are so exciting that it will rapidly gain ground, and deserves a prominent place in any toolkit aimed at understanding the nature of markets.

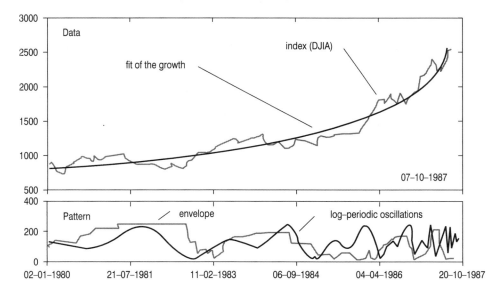

Figure 6.31   Log-periodic crash detection
Source: Reproduced from Vandewaller *et al.* (1999).

Table 6.9 Log-periodic critical crashes

Market	Period
DJIA/S&P500	29, early 37, mid-46, 87, 98
NASDAQ	00
Hang Seng Index	Oct 71, Feb 73, Sep 78, Nov 80, Oct 87, Apr 89, Jan 94, Oct 97
Russia	98
Argentina	91, 92, 94, 97
Brazil	97
Chile	91, 93
Mexico	94, 97
Peru	93
Venezuela	97
Indonesia	94
Malaysia	94
Philippines	94
Thailand	94
¥/€	Jan 00
$/€	Oct 00
ChF/$	85
DM/$	85
C$/$	98
$/¥	98

6.10   CONCLUSIONS

We have tried to show ways in which we might improve the asset allocation decision-making process. We have shown the problems with using the simplest popular measures such as the dividend yield. We have suggested some alternatives such as simple but reasonably effective models of the equity risk premium. Perhaps most interestingly we have explored some non-standard tools for asset allocation. In particular, we suggest monitoring activity in the primary markets as a good guide to investors' enthusiasm for stocks. We have also introduced some very new ideas from the emerging field of phynance (or econophysics, if you prefer). These tools are designed to seek out complex adaptive systems moving into a critical state. Early results suggest that they could be the best method of timing the market yet.

7

Corporate Finance

7.1 INTRODUCTION

Perhaps the least explored implications of the behavioural approach are those related to the corporate finance arena. This omission is all the stranger for the fact that one of the classical references to empirical corporate finance (Lintner, 1956) has a distinctly behavioural flavour. Remember that such classic constructs as Modigliani and Miller's capital structure and dividend irrelevance theorems are based on the precept of market efficiency. We hope the reader will feel that we have provided enough evidence to suggest that market efficiency is perhaps not the best paradigm for thinking about real-world financial situations. Hence the foundations of corporate finance need to be rebuilt from a behavioural standpoint.

There are essentially two approaches to issues in corporate finance stemming from the behavioural approach. The first is to assume that managers of corporations are subject to exactly the same psychological biases that we outlined in Chapter 1 (rational markets, irrational managers). The other is to model the managers of corporates as rational, and use their rationality to exploit the opportunities created by mispricing in the markets (rational manager, irrational markets). We will examine both approaches, as they offer insights into different components of corporate finance.

7.2 IRRATIONAL MANAGERS/RATIONAL MARKETS

The most relevant psychological biases in the context of management are over-optimism and over-confidence. Weinstein (1980) finds optimism is at its peak when people are dealing with situations they feel they can control. He also finds that people are more optimistic when they are very close to a project (i.e. they feel committed).

Choi and Ziebart (2000) show that in their sample of managers' forecasts for US firms between 1993 and 1998, two distinct patterns emerge. Firstly, directly ahead of a year end managers become pessimistic — presumably as an attempt to guide down market expectations. However, at everything over an eight month time horizon, managers' forecasts are unambiguously optimistic. Irani (2000) looks at 267 US management earnings forecasts between 1990 and 1995, and once again the managers appear to be seriously over-confident in their expectations.

Heaton (1998) explores the implications of managerial over-optimism for corporate finance. He finds that using a model where managers are too optimistic about the future leads to the resolution of several puzzles that plague the standard approach.

7.2.1 Pecking Order of Capital Structure Preferences

The pecking order of capital structure preferences suggests that there is an asymmetry between managers and owners. This asymmetry of information leads to a firm's securities being undervalued. External funds are less desirable because informational asymmetries between management and investors imply that external funds are undervalued in relation to the degree of asymmetry (Myers and Majluf, 1984). Hence, firms will be drawn towards internal financing wherever it is practicable. If they are forced to use external funds, they prefer to use debt, convertible securities and, as a last resort, equity. Graham and Harvey (2001) find evidence amongst CFOs of a pecking order amongst financing choices.

If the managers of a firm are permanently optimistic, they will perceive that an efficient market is undervaluing their traded securities — let alone an inefficient market! For instance, the Q2 2000 FEI survey carried out by Duke University found that no less than 82% of financial executives thought the stock market was undervaluing their equity! (See Figure 7.1.)

7.2.2 Cash Flows and Investment

Traditional theories of corporate finance have trouble explaining the positive relationship found between cash flow and investment. However, it stems from the pecking order of capital structure preferences outlined above. Managers may reject projects — even if they have a positive net present value — if they don't have sufficient internal funds. Thus when free cash flow is high, managers will find it easy to accept projects — creating a positive correlation between cash flows and investment.

7.2.3 Free Cash Flows can be Dangerous

According to Harford (1999) cash-rich firms destroy 7 cents of corporate value for every dollar of cash reserves held. The mechanism for this share holder value destruction seems to be diversification. Diversification across industries is punished by investors. As an article from the July 25 2000 *FT* put it 'Procter and Gamble was widely reported to be considering a bid for Warner–Lambert (eventually acquired by Pfizer, creating the world's largest pharmaceuticals company by market capitalization). The big institutional investors criticized Procter and Gamble, and reports that P&G was

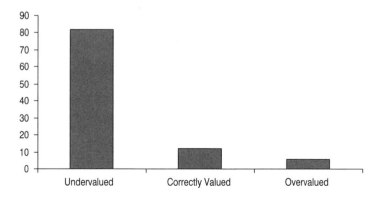

Figure 7.1   FEI survey: Q2 2000 'Do you think your stock is ...'

considering diversification sent the stock into a tailspin. Procter and Gamble decided not to diversify' (Figure 7.2).

In the US, conglomerates tend to find that they trade at a 15% discount to a basket of niche-focused firms operating in each of the individual markets. According to Lins and Servaes (1999), a similar pattern is found in both Japan and the UK. In Japan, a discount of 10% on conglomerates was found, in the UK this penalty rose to 15% (Figure 7.3).

This appears to be at odds with much of corporate and investment advice dispensed during the 1980s. Then big was beautiful, and conglomerates were the market's darlings. Here were firms that took a single proven management team and used its expertise across business ventures. Diversification was good, it smoothed out fluctuations in the earnings profiles of firms. Reducing volatility of earnings in turn reduced the firms' cost of capital — oh how times change!

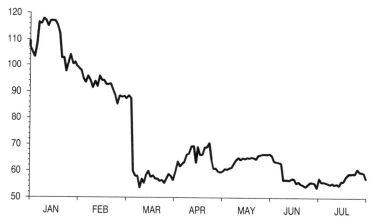

Figure 7.2   Procter and Gamble flirt with diversification
Source: Datastream.

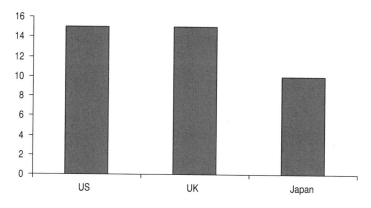

Figure 7.3   The diversification discount

Servaes (1996) looks at the pricing of diversified firms in the 1960s and 1970s in order to assess how the market treatment of conglomerates has altered over time. Interestingly, Servaes found that in the 1960s, diversified firms traded at the same level of discount that is seen today — roughly 15%. However, this discount narrowed to virtually zero in the early and mid-1970s. This is yet more evidence that equity markets are prone to fads and fashions. Perhaps the life cycle style investing model of Barberis and Shleifer (2001) could be used to explore this issue.

Optimistic managers will be more prone to make diversifying acquisitions. Because of their innate optimism and over-confidence, managers will overestimate future cash flows from the acquisition. Indeed Kaplan and Ruback (1995) show that amongst their sample of 51 highly leveraged transactions between 1983 and 1989, realized earnings before interest, tax, depreciation and amortization (EBITDA) levels are a median 3.7% and 14.4% lower than managers had forecast in years one and two respectively.

A reliance on external finance can deter managers from the pursuit of such folly. However, when sufficient funds are available internally, there is nothing to stop the over-enthusiastic manager from acting on his beliefs. Hence surplus cash flow can lead to value destruction.

Moreover, there is no reason to believe that managers will in general learn not to be optimistic. Kahneman and Lovallo (1993) show that learning normally occurs when repeated frequent similar situations occur, and there is a clear feedback between actions and results. However, corporate structure, takeovers and dividend policy decisions are infrequent and the feedback is usually delayed and noisy. Thus the opportunities for learning are greatly reduced.

Of course, in an efficient (Darwinian) market, such behaviour would be relatively swiftly eradicated. However, as the main thrust has hopefully shown, markets simply aren't efficient. As we showed in Chapter 2, we have a hard enough time keeping dual listed securities in line, let alone claiming efficiency with respect to the market for takeovers. After all the market for corporate control incurs very high transaction costs, not to mention massive amounts of idiosyncratic risk.

7.2.4 Corporate Governance

Kahneman and Lovallo (1993) suggest that managerial optimism is best controlled by the introduction of an outside viewpoint. This provides a behavioural rationale for corporate governance. If 'insiders' are overly optimistic, then in order to prevent the value destruction outlined above, 'outsiders' need to be able to extract surplus cash before it can be diverted.

The McKinsey Quarterly (Q3 2000) provided a timely example of the wide regard with which institutional investors are now holding corporate governance. They conducted a survey of some 200 fund management groups, with an estimated $3.25 trillion in assets under management. Three quarters of those surveyed said they thought corporate governance was at least as important as financial performance when evaluating companies for investment.

The survey went on to ask if two companies were fundamentally the same, i.e. in the same line of business with the same financing arrangements, but differed in terms of their commitment to corporate governance, how much of a premium would you be prepared to pay for the company with 'good' governance.

The McKinsey survey defined 'good' corporate governance as one with a majority of outside directors with no management ties to its board, that undertook formal evaluation of directors, and was responsive to requests from investors for information on governance issues. Directors should also hold significant numbers of shares in the company, with a large element of their remuneration in the form of stock options.

Figures 7.4–7.6 show the extent of the premiums that fund managers said they would be prepared to pay for a company with 'good' corporate governance. A strong correlation with the level of accounting clarity and the strength of the legal system is immediately apparent from the results. A well-governed company in Venezuela commands a 28% premium, whereas in the US a well-governed company enjoys investors' favours to the tune of 18%.

LaPorta *et al.* point out that in many countries certain share holders are much closer to the company than others. They term the managers and these controlling share holders as insiders, with the minority share holders as outsiders.

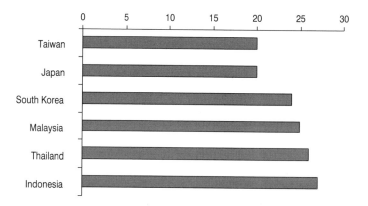

Figure 7.4   Corporate governance premium — Asia

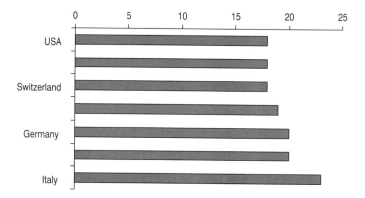

Figure 7.5   Corporate governance premium — Europe, US

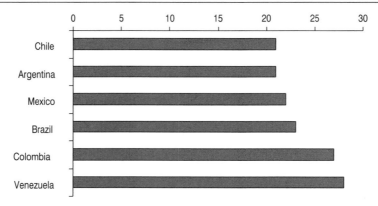

Figure 7.6   Corporate governance premium — Latin America

Corporate governance is essentially a set of mechanisms which help the outsiders prevent the insiders from various forms of expropriation. Expropriation can range from simply stealing cash to transfer pricing and investor dilution.

Managers may deliberately create complex structures in order to achieve their aims. Mayer (1999) highlights the example of Unilever. Unilever comprises Unilever N.V. (the Dutch part) and Unilever PLC (the UK part). They trade as a single entity. This is achieved through two holding companies, N.V. Elma and United Holdings Limited, which in turn are held by the Unilever companies and have cross-share holdings in each other. They in turn hold the special shares and deferred stock in Unilever N.V. and PLC respectively. The significance of these special shares and deferred stock is that they nominate people for election as members of the boards of N.V. and PLC. In other words, elections to the board of Unilever are by two companies owned by Unilever!

Figure 7.7 shows one measure of how important insiders may potentially be. It shows the percentage of votes cast by the largest voting block. For instance, in Austria the

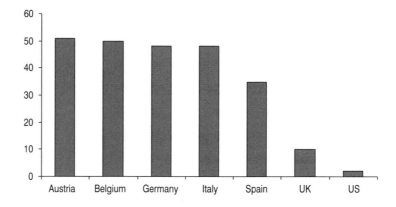

Figure 7.7   Percentage of votes cast by the largest voting block (median)

average largest voting block is a staggering 52%. In the UK it is just 10%, and in the US it is below the minimum disclosure level of 5%. The need for corporate governance is at its strongest where the concentration of voting is at its narrowest.

Gompers, Ishii and Metrick (2001) build a 'Governance Index' for about 1500 firms per year, and then study the relationship between this index and several forward-looking performance measures during the 1990s. They find a striking relationship between corporate governance and stock returns. An investment strategy that bought the firms in the lowest decile of the index (strongest share holder rights) and sold the firms in the highest decile of the index (weakest share holder rights) would have earned abnormal[1] returns of 8.5% per year during the sample period. Gompers, Ishii and Metrick also find that weaker share holder rights are associated with lower profits, lower sales growth, higher capital expenditures and a higher amount of corporate acquisitions.

7.2.5 Dividends as an Extraction Mechanism

Dividends can also be explained within this framework. Way back in the late 1950s Modigliani and Miller proved that in a taxless efficient markets world, a company's dividend decision should not matter to investors. Because income is usually taxed at a higher rate than capital gains, in a world with taxes, investors should actually prefer capital gains to dividends. So why do firms pay dividends?

Over the years economists have proposed many potential solutions to the 'dividend puzzle'. Many suggested that firms signal future profitability by paying dividends. However, Benartzi, Michaely and Thaler (1997) show that firms will increase their dividends after a few years of good growth. But that is uncorrelated with future operating performance. That is to say, dividends reflect the past not the future.

In the context of the struggle between insiders and outsiders, dividends can be seen as a mechanism whereby the outsiders extract surplus cash before the insiders divert it to wasteful ends. In traditional agency models, the managers of the firm are motivated by such things as empire building, and act deliberately against the share holders' best interests. In our view of the world, we don't require 'evil' managers driven by a desire to empire build — which incidentally has little, if any, empirical support. Rather in our model, managers are just overly optimistic and overly confident — a fact supported by a wealth of psychological studies.

7.3 RATIONAL MANAGERS/IRRATIONAL MARKETS

The previous section dealt with cases where managers were modelled as irrational, but markets were generally assumed to be rational. In this section we reverse these assumptions, and assume that managers are by and large rational creatures, but markets are irrational. Thus we explore how firms effectively seek to arbitrage against market mispricing of their stock. Given this role, we will be focusing on firms' decisions to issue equity. Thus mergers, acquisitions, IPOs, SEOs and repurchases are all basically seen as attempts by firms to arbitrage against a perceived mispricing. After all

---

[1] After FF3 with WML.

the act of equity issuance is the creation of a very close (if not perfect) substitute for the already listed equity. Recall from Chapter 2 that the lack of ability to create close substitutes was one of the factors that bedeviled arbitrageurs in the market.

7.3.1 Mergers and Acquisitions

The global trend of corporate growth through acquisition continues largely unchecked (Table 7.1). A staggering 25,207 deals occurred in 2000, with an aggregate value of no less than $3062bn.

Whilst this is undoubtedly great news for investment banks, how does it fit with the mantra of increasing share holder value? Debates over how to measure the impact of events such as mergers and acquisitions on long-run performance still rage (Barber and Lyon, 1999; Mitchell and Stafford, 2001). The basic concern stems from all tests of long-term abnormal returns being joint tests of stock market efficiency and a model of equilibrium asset pricing. Obviously, this is not a problem for studies of short-term returns, because virtually all models of equilibrium asset pricing predict a zero return over 1–3 day time horizons. However, 3–5 year estimates of expected returns can vary widely depending upon the model used. Against benchmark imprecision it is exceptionally hard to judge the statistical significance of reported abnormal returns.

However, given the dominance of the market efficiency school, the burden of proof falls on the behavioural school. For instance, using an FF3 + WML asset pricing model as the benchmark for rational asset pricing seems distinctly unfair, given that as we showed in Chapter 4 most of the evidence suggests behavioural factors at work in HML and WML in particular. Indeed Loughran and Ritter (2000) aptly refer to such benchmarks as the uniformly least powerful tests of market efficiency. In general, a standard appears to be emerging around the use of buy-and-hold returns because they duplicate 'real'-world investment strategies. However, the idea of matching sample firms with other firms based on size and price to book has also found much sympathy within the academic environment.

In order to try and illustrate the strength of the behavioural approach we will use the most stringent criteria whenever possible, effectively taking the fight on in the way which favours the efficient markets view the most. For instance, Table 7.2 shows the three year abnormal returns following mergers and acquisitions based on the work of Mitchell and Stafford (2001).

Table 7.1   Stylized facts US M&A 1973–1998

	1973–1979	1980–1989	1990–1998
Number	789	1427	2040
All cash	38.3%	45.3%	27.4%
All stock	37.0%	32.9%	57.8%
Any stock	45.1%	45.6%	70.9%
Premium (median)	47.2%	37.7%	34.5%
Own industry	29.9%	40.1%	47.8%

Source: Adapted from Andrade, Mitchell and Stafford (2001).

Table 7.2 Three year post-merger abnormal returns for acquiring firms (1961–1993)

Portfolio composition	Equal weighted	Value weighted
Full sample	−5.0% **	−1.4%
Financed with stock	−9.0% **	−4.3%
Financed without stock	−1.4%	3.6%
Growth firms	−6.5%	−7.2%
Value firms	−2.9%	1.1%

**Denotes statistical significance at the 1% level.

When considering the equal-weighted sample (i.e. all firms are equally important regardless of market capitalization) the data show that mergers are generally value-destructive, especially when they are financed with stock. When considering the value-weighted sample (i.e. market capitalization weighted) the effects still have the same sign, but are not statistically significant, suggesting that the effects causing under-performance are highly concentrated in small stocks.

Of course, in real-world investing we don't have the luxury of being able to debate the academic niceties of statistical significance. Instead we are forced to use the best available evidence to provide heuristics (rules of thumb) that will not lead us too far astray. To this end it seems reasonable to say that in general mergers aren't good news for long-term investors, and this is especially true of mergers and acquisitions conducted by growth firms and paid for in stock.

Observational equivalence is the name given by economists to situations where two theories essentially predict the same outcome. Mergers and acquisitions tend to fall into this camp. Both the irrational manager/rational market and rational manager/irrational market approaches can explain the stylized facts surrounding M&A activity.

The links between mergers and acquisitions and the dangers of diversification outlined above should be clear. One of the most obvious ways in which an overly optimistic manager might try to extend his empire is through acquisition. Over-optimistic, over-confident managers may well believe in their own ability to run other firms too much. But as we noted earlier, these same managers are also likely to exhibit pecking order capital structure preferences, so how do we reconcile the high percentage of stock-financed mergers with the fact that these overly optimistic managers habitually believe that their equity is undervalued by the market?

If managers have pecking order capital structure preferences, then mergers and acquisitions that are stock-financed must be perceived as exceptionally good value. This can occur in two situations, when the projects really are very good, and when managerial perceptions are especially wrong and the project is actually very bad. If projects are actually good then it seems likely that managers should be able to access other preferred sources of financing, in particular debt. Thus, acquisitions financed by equity are more likely to be bad purchases.

The managerial optimism hypothesis predicts that equity-financed takeovers should have worse announcement day returns than takeovers financed with internal funds or debt (in terms of the acquirer firm). Table 7.3 is again taken from Mitchell and Stafford

Table 7.3 Announcement abnormal returns (US, 1973–1998)

	Stock	No stock
Target firm		
$(-1, +1)$	13.0%	20.1%
$(-20, \text{close})$	20.8%	27.8%
Acquirer firm		
$(-1, +1)$	-1.5%	0.4%
$(-20, \text{close})$	-6.3%	-0.2%

Reproduced from Mitchell and Stafford, Managerial Decisions and Long Term Stock Price Performance, Journal of Business, (2001), with permission of the University of Chicago.

(2001), using the harshest methodology possible. It confirms the prediction just made on the impact of financing on announcement period returns.

Two different measures of announcement returns are calculated. The first row in each case is labelled $(-1, +1)$ and represents a three day event window around the announcement. However, as we showed in Chapter 2, merger arbitrage is a risky business, thus to completely incorporate the market impact, we also show an expanded event window beginning 20 days before the announcement, and ending at the close of the deal. In both sets of announcement returns, the performance is noticeably worse where stock financing is being used by the acquirer.

However, it is equally possible that the long-run underperformance of stock-financed acquisitions results from rational corporate managers reacting to and exploiting market misvaluation of their equity. Remember a stock-financed acquisition can really be seen as the combination of two events, firstly an equity issue and then a purchase. So it can be seen as the firm trying to arbitrage against a stock market that is valuing its equity too highly.

Shleifer and Vishny (2001) present a model that will undoubtedly become a corner stone of the behavioural theory of corporate finance. They present a model in which corporate managers seek to exploit market mispricings in the realm of mergers and acquisitions. Their model offers a number of interesting predictions, including: (i) acquisitions are disproportionately for stock when market valuations are high, and for cash when they are low; (ii) targets in cash acquisitions earn low returns prior to the acquisitions, whereas bidders in stock acquisitions earn high returns; (iii) long-run returns to bidders in stock acquisitions are likely to be negative, those to bidders in cash acquisitions are likely to be positive. A quick glance at the empirical evidence outlined above confirms these predictions match the patterns observed in the market.

More controversially, the Shleifer and Vishny model also suggests that diversified acquisitions may be in the interests of share holders despite the negative returns. Perhaps it is optimal for managers and share holders to use overvalued equity as a currency in transactions to buy less (but still) overvalued firms, thereby obtaining some real capital with a cheap source of financing. For example, AOL acquiring Time Warner. The alternative could be worse, when the market eventually realizes the firm's stock is overvalued then it might fall even further than it does post-acquisition. This is of course a counterfactual statement, and thus very difficult to test, but future research must surely be directed towards this area if we are to gain a better understanding of the M&A process.

We will now turn to other (clearer) instances where corporates effectively act as arbitrageurs against their own share price in the market.

7.3.2 Initial Public Offerings

Probably the most transparent equity issuance occurrence is that of IPOs, the first time a company lists on the stock exchange. This event therefore offers us an ideal spring board to explore the role of rational managers exploiting market mispricing. Before we begin this exploration, a little more depth on the notion of 'rational managers' may be worthwhile. Often in the literature it is assumed that such managers are omniscient creatures, capable of timing the market to perfection. Over the years, having met a large number of corporate managers, I am willing to refute this description. Most of the corporate managers I have met are generally as bemused about the stock market as the rest of us.

So what do we mean, when we talk of rational managers? In many ways this is short hand for the interaction of corporate finance/broking departments, markets and firms. The real engine for driving IPOs is the demand side, not the supply side. Investors clamouring for new stock drives corporate finance departments to go and find firms that need financing, and bring them to market. However, for the sake of ease, we will refer to this as the 'rational manager approach'.

We have noted several times before that IPOs move in cyclical patterns, and that they tend to cluster around market peaks. However, here we will go much deeper into the issues surrounding IPOs. Regardless of the country under consideration, IPO markets tend to exhibit three key features:

- Initial underpricing
- Hot markets
- Long-run underperformance

Let us examine each of these in turn.

7.3.2.1 Initial Underpricing

One of the most stable patterns observed in the market for IPOs is that there is a large initial return. That is to say there is a large price gap between the offer price and the price at the end of the first day of trading. This represents a significant difference of opinion between the investment bank who prices the issue and the value that the stock market (investors) is willing to put on the stock. As Table 7.4 shows, virtually every market in the world seems to exhibit this pattern.

The scale of the initial underpricing varies from market to market, and varies over time. In the US, the average initial underpricing return for IPOs listing between 1960 and 1996 was 16%. Between 1996 and 2000, the average initial return soared to 37%. (See Figure 7.8.)

Whilst on average there are positive initial returns on IPOs, there is also a wide distribution over individual issues. Figure 7.9 shows the distribution of first day returns

Table 7.4 Average initial returns for 38 countries

Country	Source	Sample Size	Time Period	Average initial return
Australia	Lee, Taylor & Walter; Woo	381	1976–1995	12.1%
Austria	Aussenegg	76	1984–1999	6.5%
Belgium	Rogiers, Manigart & Ooghe; Manigart	86	1984–1999	14.6%
Brazil	Aggarwal, Leal & Hernandez	62	1979–1990	78.5%
Canada	Jog & Riding; Jog & Srivastava; Kryzanowski & Rakita	500	1971–1999	6.3%
Chile	Aggarwal, Leal & Hernandez; Celis & Maturana	55	1982–1997	8.8%
China	Datar & Mao; Gu & Qin (A shares)	432	1990–2000	256.9%
Denmark	Jakobsen & Sorensen	117	1984–1998	5.4%
Finland	Keloharju; Westerholm	99	1984–1997	10.1%
France	Husson & Jacquillat; Leleux & Muzyka; Paliard & Belletante; Derrien & Womack	448	1983–1998	9.5%
Germany	Ljungqvist	407	1978–1999	27.7%
Greece	Kazantzis & Thomas	129	1987–1994	51.7%
Hong Kong	McGuinness; Zhao & Wu	334	1980–1996	15.9%
India	Krishnamurti & Kumar	98	1992–1993	35.3%
Indonesia	Hanafi	106	1989–1994	15.1%
Israel	Kandel, Sarig & Wohl	28	1993–1994	4.5%
Italy	Arosio, Giudici & Paleari	164	1985–2000	23.9%
Japan	Fukuda; Dawson & Hiraki; Hebner & Hiraki; Hamao, Packer & Ritter, Kaneko & Pettway	1542	1970–2000	26.4%
Korea	Dhatt, Kim & Lim; Ihm; Choi & Heo	477	1980–1996	74.3%
Malaysia	Isa; Isa & Yong	401	1980–1998	104.1%
Mexico	Aggarwal, Leal & Hernandez	37	1987–1990	33.0%
Netherlands	Wessels; Eijgenhuijsen & Buijs; Ljungqvist, Jenkinson & Wilhelm	143	1982–1999	10.2%
New Zealand	Vos & Cheung; Camp & Munro	201	1979–1999	23.0%
Nigeria	Ikoku	63	1989–1993	19.1%
Norway	Emilsen, Pedersen & Saettern	68	1984–1996	12.5%
Philippines	Sullivan & Unite	104	1987–1997	22.7%
Poland	Aussenegg	149	1991–1998	35.6%
Portugal	Almeida & Duque	21	1992–1998	10.6%
Singapore	Lee, Taylor & Walter	128	1973–1992	31.4%
South Africa	Page & Reyneke	118	1980–1991	32.7%
Spain	Ansotegui & Fabregat	99	1986–1998	10.7%
Sweden	Rydqvist	251	1980–1994	34.1%
Switzerland	Kunz & Aggarwal	42	1983–1989	35.8%
Taiwan	Lin & Sheu; Liaw, Liu & Wei	293	1986–1998	31.1%
Thailand	Wethyavivorn & Koo-smith; Lonkani & Tirapat	292	1987–1997	46.7%

Table 7.4   *Continued*

Country	Source	Sample Size	Time Period	Average initial return
Turkey	Kiymaz	138	1990–1996	13.6%
United Kingdom	Dimson; Levis; Ljungqvist	3042	1959–2000	17.5%
United States	Ibbotson, Sindelar & Ritter	14760	1960–2000	18.4%

See references listed at http://bear.cba.ufl.edu/ritter/interntl.htm. Where more than one set of authors is listed as a source of information, a combined sample has been constructed. Average initial returns are constructed in different manners from study to study, although all weight each IPO equally. In general, in countries where market prices are available immediately after offerings, the one-day raw return (offer price to close) is reported. In countries where there is a delay before unconstrained market prices are reported, market-adjusted returns over an interval of several weeks are reported.

Source: Reprinted from 'Investment banking and securities issuance', J. Ritter, Copyright (2001), with permission from Elsevier Science.

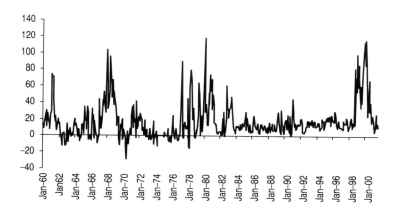

Figure 7.8   US initial returns

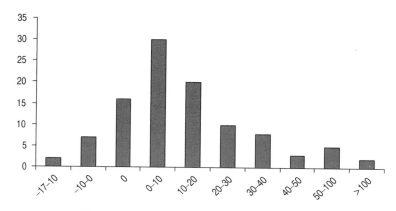

Figure 7.9   Distribution of US initial returns

for US IPOs from 1990 to 1996. As Ritter (1998) points out, one in 11 IPOs has a negative initial return, and one in six closes at the offer price.

The price charged by investment bankers to ensure the offer is taken up is significantly lower than the price that investors attach to the issue. Multiplying the initial return by the number of shares issued gives the money left on the table by the investment bankers. Ritter and Loughran (2001) show that the average US IPO left $9m on the table. Between 1990 and 1998, investment banks in the US alone left a staggering $27bn on the table. This is more than double the $13 billion in fees that were generated from the same transactions!

Our work on the UK shows similar patterns. In our sample covering UK IPOs during 1991 to 2000, the average initial return was 28%. Breaking the full sample into two sub-samples reveals that the average initial return between 1991 and 1996 was a relatively paltry 7.5%. However, in the post-1996 period, this average return rose dramatically to 29% (Figure 7.10).

As with the US sample, UK initial returns show a wide distribution. Figure 7.11 shows the distribution of UK initial returns between 1991 and 2000. One in eight IPOs has a negative return, one in nine closes at the offer price on the first day of trading, and one in 10 generates an initial return of more than 50%.

In terms of money left on the table, the average IPO shows a £3 million difference between the investment banker's valuation and the stock market valuation. Between 1996 and 2000, investment banks handling UK new issues have left a total of £2.7 billion on the table.

Why are new issues underpriced? There are a number of potential (non-mutually exclusive) explanations for the underpricing phenomenon.

    I. The winner's curse.

       Investors are frequently at an informational disadvantage when it comes to IPOs. Some IPOs are lemons,[2] this creates an adverse selection problem. Are you looking

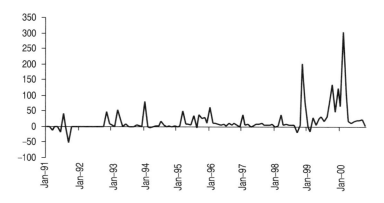

Figure 7.10   UK initial returns

---

[2] A lemon is a US term for a car which has been welded together from at least two cars. On the surface it is virtually impossible to distinguish lemons from genuine used cars.

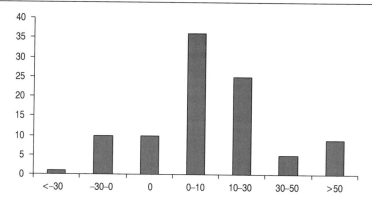

Figure 7.11   Distribution of UK initial returns

at a good IPO or a bad IPO? Faced with this problem investors will only buy IPOs if they are underpriced in general to compensate them for the risk of picking a bad one.

An alternative is that investors are tempted into holding IPOs vis-à-vis other equities. Why buy an IPO when you can buy an equity that is already trading? After all the listed firm has already gone through the trials and tribulations of being an IPO. It now has a history of earnings and stock market performance, so investors at least have some idea of what they are buying into. The high initial return may be seen as the amount required to tempt risk-averse investors into taking the chance on an unproven stock rather than a listed one.

II. The market feedback hypothesis.

When investment bankers use book building, underpricing may be used to encourage investors to reveal information during the marketing round — low balling the estimate to tempt investors to reveal their own true estimate of the company's value. This suggests a testable prediction: there will only be partial adjustment of the offer price shown in the first prospectus to that in the final filing. That is to say IPOs whose price is revised upwards from that in the initial prospectus will enjoy higher first day returns than those whose price is revised downwards. Such trends certainly emerge in the US data (Table 7.5).

Table 7.5   US IPOs 1990–1996

	All	Offer price < min price in the original filing	Offer price in the middle of the original range	Offer price > max price in the original filing
Average initial return		3.5%	12%	30%
No. of IPOs	2861	708	1511	642

Source: Barry, Gilson and Ritter (1998).

III. The bandwagon hypothesis.
   If investors pay attention not only to their own demand for an IPO, but also to
   other investors' demands, then bandwagon effects may be created. If an investor
   sees a company that no one else wants to buy, she may decide not to invest, even
   though she has a favourable impression. In order to overcome this, the issuer may
   wish to underprice. This may encourage initial investors to buy, and hence create
   favourable bandwagon effects.
IV. The signalling hypothesis.
   Investors like underpriced new issues. This creates a feeling of goodwill, which can
   be used to show placing power in other subsequent IPOs. The investment bank
   gradually builds a reputation in the market for IPOs. The most important aspect of
   pricing becomes simply getting the deal away, banking a fee not maximizing it is
   the driving factor. In other words, from the investment bank perspective, an IPO is
   a binary event — it either goes or it doesn't. The philosophy of the investment
   bank is that it is better to secure a fee x with high probability of success, rather
   than x plus with a lower certainty of success.

7.3.2.2   Hot Markets

A distinct cyclical pattern exists in both the initial returns from IPOs and the volume of
IPOs brought to the market (Figure 7.12). Periods of rising initial returns and
increasing numbers of deals are known as hot markets. IPO hot markets seem to follow
periods of high stock market returns. As we showed in Chapter 5, there may even be a
case for incorporating the information generated in the asset allocation process.

   What causes this clustering of IPOs? Graham and Harvey (2001) conducted a
massive survey of USA Inc. in order to try and uncover the answer to a number of
riddles in corporate finance. Figure 7.13 shows the findings with regard to which
factors are important in the decision to issue equity. Of the top three most cited factors

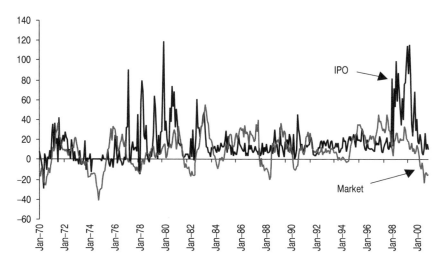

Figure 7.12   US initial returns and market returns

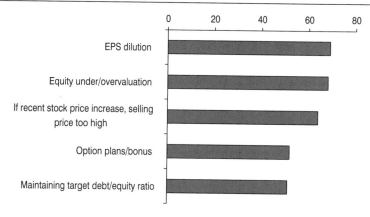

Figure 7.13   The decision to issue equity is influenced by

influencing the decision to issue equity two are related to market levels, so to some extent our ideas of managers deliberately trying to time the market seem to hold water empirically.

As we saw in Chapter 2, in markets with restricted short selling, it is the optimists that set the price. Nowhere is this more true than in the IPO market. Remember we showed that IPO stocks are particularly 'special' in the stock lending market. In addition, such rules as NASD Rule 3370 require brokers to guarantee delivery of borrowed shares before allowing customers to sell short, and few brokerage firms or institutional investors will lend IPO shares to short sellers. The Securities Exchange Commission also prohibits firms in the underwriting syndicate from loaning allocated shares until 30 days after the IPO. Therefore, initial IPO prices may not reflect the sentiment of the most pessimistic investors.

Houge *et al.* (2001) use three proxies for the divergence of opinion in order to see if prices really are determined by optimists, the percentage opening bid–ask spread, the time of the first trade and the flipping ratio. These variables respectively describe the uncertainty faced by a wide spectrum of IPO participants: market makers, underwriters and institutional investors. Houge *et al.* find that IPOs with a wide initial spread, a late opening trade and/or a high proportion of institutional flipping exhibit poor long-term returns. This will be important in analysing the long-run returns to IPO investing (see below). But for now we will take this as firm evidence that initial returns are governed by the degree of investor enthusiasm for the stock.

Lowry (2001) examines the causes of fluctuations in the level of IPOs. She finds that there are two particularly important factors in determining when firms choose to go public. Firstly, Lowry finds that much of the intertemporal variation in aggregate IPO volume reflects variation in private firms' demand for capital. IPO volume is higher when economic conditions are strong and there are more real investment opportunities. The second factor that Lowry identifies as especially important is investor demand. The significance of investor sentiment proxies indicates that a disproportionate number of firms go public when they are especially highly valued by the market. She notes that firms that go public during high-volume periods (hot markets) do not appear to be overvalued relative to other similar firms; it appears that these firms successfully go public when their entire sector is overvalued. Schill (2000) finds similar results, although he notes that managers seem to have both market and industry timing ability.

7.3.2.3 Long-run Underperformance

The third and final pattern associated with the IPO market has already been alluded to above, it is the long-run underperformance of new issues — measured from the closing price of the first day of trading. Because we are once again dealing with long horizon returns, many of the same issues discussed in Section 7.3.1 come up once again.

Table 7.6 shows the annual return on US IPOs in the five years post-issuance, along with benchmarks based on market capitalization (size-matched) and market capitalization and price to book (style-matched). It shows that US IPOs have underperformed other firms of the same size by an average 3.4% per year during the five years post-issuance. When a style benchmark is used (i.e. accounting for both size and price to book) there is an excess performance of 0.2% per year for the IPOs.

However, as Brav, Geczy and Gompers (2000) show most IPOs fall in the extreme small growth category. Whether or not they issue, firms in this style group have witnessed extremely low returns for the last several decades. However, it is hard to imagine that this finding will continue to hold once the internet bubble enters the long-run performance data.

Once again a similar pattern is observed in the international data (Table 7.7), long-run underperformance seems to be yet another constant feature of the IPOs regardless of location.

The key reason for this long-run underperformance seems to be intimately related to causes of hot markets. As we noted above, there is considerable evidence that suggests firms try to time their equity issuance. If there are periods when investors are especially optimistic about stocks (after a period of high broad market returns if investors are myopic and look at the recent past as a guide to the immediate future, say) then large cycles in IPO volumes may represent firms trying to exploit this source of 'cheap finance'.

Table 7.6 Percentage returns on US IPOs (1970–1998) during the first five years post-issue

	First six months	Second six months	First year	Second year	Third year	Fourth year	Fifth year	Geometric mean years 1–5
IPO firms	6.2	2.6	9.2	8.5	10.4	13.7	12.1	10.7
Size-matched	4.5	5.9	10.8	14.1	14.2	17.2	14.0	14.1
Difference	1.7	−3.3	−1.6	−5.6	−3.8	−3.5	−1.9	−3.4
IPO firms	6.8	2.9	10.1	11.5	11.4	12.6	9.7	11.0
Style-matched	2.2	4.4	6.7	12.4	11.2	13.1	10.8	10.8
Difference	4.6	−1.5	3.4	−0.9	0.2	−0.5	−1.1	0.2

Source: Reprinted from 'Investment banking and securities issuance', J. Ritter, Copyright (2001), with permission from Elsevier Science.

Table 7.7   Global markets: long-run IPO underperformance

Country	Sample size	Time period	Long-run underperformance
Australia	266	1976–1989	−46.5
Austria	67	1964–1996	−27.3
Brazil	62	1979–1990	−47.0
Canada	258	1971–1992	−17.9
Chile	19	1982–1990	−23.7
Finland	85	1984–1992	−21.1
Germany	170	1978–1992	−12.1
Japan	975	1970–1996	−27.0
Singapore	128	1973–1992	−9.2
United Kingdom	588	1985–1992	−15.0
United States	13,308	1960–1999	−20.0

Source: Ritter (1998).

The windows of opportunity hypothesis predicts that those firms going public in the highest volume period are likely to be more overvalued than other IPOs. There should be a correlation between high-volume periods and lowest long-run returns. This pattern does indeed exist in almost all the data sets (although it should be noted that the relationship is not necessarily linear).

Remember we pointed out that in markets with limited short selling and heterogeneous beliefs amongst investors, it will be the optimistic investors that determine market price (Miller, 1977). As more information becomes available about a firm's performance over time, the divergence of beliefs will be reduced, and the marginal investor will no longer be so overly optimistic, eventually leading to a correction in performance.

Rajan and Servaes (1997) show that these patterns certainly exist amongst analysts. Analysts covering IPOs are almost universally too optimistic about the firm's future earnings ability. Table 7.8 shows just how easy it may be for investors to be overly optimistic about IPOs. After five years on average just 61.4% of each year's IPOs are still active. Almost 22% of all IPOs have either been liquidated, or disappeared through unknown causes after five years.

Table 7.8   The fate of US IPOs (%) (1975–1995)

Reference point	Active	Mergers	Exchanges	Liquidations	Unknown
Year 1	98.6	0.5	0.1	0.6	0.3
Year 2	90.5	3.7	0.3	4.2	1.3
Year 3	81.1	7.4	0.5	8.6	2.4
Year 4	71.3	11.6	0.7	13.3	3.0
Year 5	61.4	15.6	1.0	18.4	3.5

7.3.2.4   A Unified Theory of the Stylized Facts on IPOs

As I was doing the research for this chapter, I came across a new paper that fits very nicely into the new behavioural corporate finance framework promoted here. Ljungqvist, Nanda and Singh (2001) present a model that appears to offer a unified framework for discussing a lot of the features of IPO markets outlined above. They note that a window of opportunity, divergence of opinion model can explain all the main features of IPO markets, and also has further (and in some cases, as of yet untested) predictions. The link between divergence of opinion and long-run under-performance has already been outlined above, and is relatively obvious. The link between divergence and short-run underpricing may be less obvious. Underwriters may underprice the issue, in order to give their regular investors an opportunity to exploit the more optimistic investors. Effectively, the underwriter transfers the risk of the issue to the institutional investors, who then pick off the irrational investors along the demand curve in the after-market. The initial underpricing is required as compensation for the risk that the hot market ends, and the institutional investors are then forced to offload their inventory at a loss. The key predictions from their model are as follows.

Prediction 1: As the difference of opinion between rational and irrational investors increases, both the offer price and the underpricing increase. This is consistent with the evidence presented in Ljungqvist, Jenkinson and Wilhelm (2001) who show that underpricing is higher, the more the offer price exceeds the midpoint of the original indicative price range. Note there is a behavioural explanation for the same fact, as in the market feedback hypothesis outlined above.

Prediction 2: The greater the difference of opinion between rational and irrational investors, the worse the long-run performance will be. Using the proxies discussed above Houge *et al.* (2001) show that long-run underperformance is clearly related to the divergence of opinion surrounding the issue (Table 7.9).

Prediction 3: As investor optimism increases, more companies will have an incentive to go public. Lowry and Schwert (2001) show that following periods of exceptionally high underpricing, both IPO volume and IPO registrations increase. They also show that firms already registered for IPO accelerate the process.

Prediction 4: As the IPO market heats up, lower quality companies are taken public, resulting in a decline in the average quality of issuers. Ritter pointed out that in 1997,

Table 7.9   Divergence of opinion indicators and IPO performance (US)

	No. of IPOs	First day return	Flipping ratio	Time of first trade	Three year returns		
					IPOs	VW index	Relative wealth
1993	513	12.4%	29.3%	10:45 am	38.7%	53.8%	0.90
1994	408	11.0%	30.0%	10:52 am	70.9%	87.0%	0.91
1995	449	20.6%	28.9%	11:03 am	22.6%	87.1%	0.66
1996	655	17.7%	31.1%	11:09 am	17.0%	82.9%	0.64
Total	2025	15.7%	29.9%	10:58 am	34.6%	77.3%	0.76

Source: Houge *et al.* (2001).

68% of firms listing in the US had track records covering 12 months of earnings. In 1999, this had collapsed to just 25% of those firms listing.

Prediction 5: As the IPO market heats up, companies are more likely to raise money for non-investment reasons, such as paying down debt. This prediction is as of yet untested.

Prediction 6: Underwriters have a strong preference for regular (institutional) investors. Empirical evidence suggests that IPOs are heavily skewed towards institutional investors (Ljungqvist and Wilhelm, 2001). Cornelli and Goldreich (2001) show that regular investors are favoured over irregular ones. Ang, Brau and Ljungqvist (2001) show that in offers that are marketed to both institutional and retail investors, the more retail demand the underwriter can generate, the more aggressively the issue is priced and so the initial underpricing is lower.

Prediction 7: Underwriters penalize investors who engage in excessive flipping. Anecdotally, this is certainly the case. Schwert (2001) shows that investors don't exploit flipping despite the obvious financial gains from doing so. He shows that $1000 invested in January 1960 in a random sample of IPOs, and then sold at the end of each month, and reinvested in another random sample the next month would have generated returns of 127×10^{33} by the end of December 2000. In contrast, $1000 invested in the value-weighted CRSP index in January 1960 would be worth $83,000 at the end of 2000. Hence by not flipping on a monthly basis investors are giving away massive alpha. The only plausible reason must be that the strategy is simply impossible in the real world, since underwriters would block such an investor from participating in future IPOs.

Prediction 8: Over time institutional investors unload their excess inventory. Hence there should be a gradual transfer of ownership from institutional investors to retail investors.

Prediction 9: Lock-up provisions (preventing insiders from selling) ensure that institutional regular investors get the opportunity to exploit the irrationally optimistic investors first. Brav and Gompers (2000) and Field and Hanka (2001) show that share prices fall significantly at the expiry of lock-up periods (to the tune of 2% in the Field and Hanka study).

Prediction 10: If the irrational demand transpires to be unexpectedly low, underwriters may engage in price-supporting activity. This clearly benefits their key regular investors, thereby protecting the ongoing nature of the relationship.

This model looks to match the empirical facts very closely, and provides a solid unified framework to understand developments in the IPO market.

7.3.3 Seasoned Equity Offerings

An SEO occurs when a firm with an existing market listing issues new shares. Numerous studies document that in the US there is an announcement effect of -3% on average for SEOs. The basic model to explain this result is one that will be familiar to readers from our earlier comments. Management are generally assumed to have information that enables them to determine whether the market price is fair or not. If it is perceived to be overvalued, then the firm's managers will seek to issue stock and take advantage of this opportunity. The market observes this fact, and interprets SEOs as a signal that management thinks its own stock is overvalued, and hence generates a negative announcement effect (Figure 7.14).

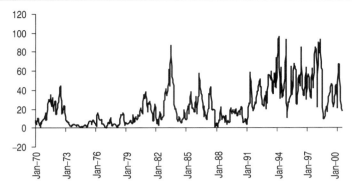

Figure 7.14   SEOs

However, it doesn't stop there. In common with much of the literature on market reactions to corporate events, the market appears to under-react to the initial event (see Kadiyala and Rau, 2001). Despite the negative reaction, the data suggests that firms that conduct SEOs actually disappoint further than the market initially expects.

Ritter and Loughran (1995) find that firms that engage in SEOs have an average return of 72% in the year prior to issuance. However, in the five years post-issue it is a very different story. Table 7.10 illustrates the picture for the 7122 SEOs conducted between 1970 and 1998; the average annual return in the five years after issuing is 10.1%. Non-issuing firms matched by market capitalization delivered an annual average return of 14.6%, leading to an underperformance of 4.5% p.a. on average for the SEO firms in the five years post-issue. See also Table 7.11.

When a style benchmark is used (matched by market capitalization and price to book), the results alter very little. The underperformance of SEOs drops slightly to 3.6% p.a. in the five year post-issue period when compared against a style benchmark. Jegadeesh (2001) goes one step further and includes a momentum portfolio (WML in

Table 7.10   Percentage returns on US SEOs (1970–1998) during the first five years post-issue

	First six months	Second six months	First year	Second year	Third year	Fourth year	Fifth year	Geometric mean years 1–5
SEO firms	6.8	2.2	9.4	4.3	9.1	13.7	14.4	10.1
Size-matched	6.1	7.0	14.1	13.0	14.2	15.6	16.1	14.6
Difference	0.7	−4.8	−4.7	−8.7	−5.1	−1.9	−1.7	−4.5
SEO firms	7.1	2.5	10.0	6.1	10.8	13.1	13.0	10.6
Style-matched	5.4	5.7	11.4	13.6	13.7	16.9	15.4	14.2
Difference	1.7	−3.2	−1.4	−7.5	−2.9	−3.8	−2.4	−3.6

Source: Reprinted from 'Investment banking and securities issuance', J. Ritter, Copyright (2001), with permission from Elsevier Science.

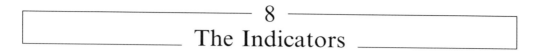

8

The Indicators

Ideas have to be wedded to actions

Henry Miller

8.1 INTRODUCTION

Throughout this book the aim has been to translate the ideas, concepts and theories of behavioural finance into practical advice and measurable variables. Due to the nature of behavioural finance, much of the work is based on outperforming in the cross-section, rather than the time series — as noted in the introductory chapter. As a result of this, many of the indicators are best built into quantitative screens, such as those outlined in Chapter 3. However, a few are suitable for use in more time series-focused work.

The behavioural approach focuses heavily on placing the market at the heart of the analysis. Much of what we have talked about elsewhere in this book is really about inferring what the market has priced in. In this chapter we try to provide a quick overview of some of the indicators that are found useful in analysing market conditions from a behavioural perspective — in general more details on these indicators can be found in the relevant chapter. This section should be thought of as a quick reference guide.

8.2 LIQUIDITY MEASURES

 I. Bond markets
   On–off the run spreads
   Commercial paper (corporate bonds) vs. government bonds
   Swap rates — government bonds: used to measure financial risk

II. Equity markets
   Bid–ask spreads
   Turnover
   Absolute price change/trading volume

8.3 SENTIMENT MEASURES

- Surveys — Merrill Lynch, II for US professionals, AAII for US individuals.
- Optimism can be proxied by the ratio of analysts' upgrades/downgrades.
- Uncertainty (heterogeneity of opinion) can be proxied by the standard deviation of analysts' forecasts.
- Put/call ratios.
- Discount to NAV on closed end funds.

- Expected volatility can be proxied by ln(VIX/sigma) where VIX is the traded option volatility and sigma is realized historical volatility.
- Implied equity risk premium.

8.4 ASSET ALLOCATION MEASURES

- Information of IPOs/equity issuance.
- M&A financing methods.
- Log-periodic signatures.
- Insider trading activity.
- Turnover.
- Payout ratio.

8.5 EARNINGS MEASURES

Two categories of earnings management techniques, income smoothing and hiding the real firm's performance, both involve the need to estimate the degree of accruals as measured by:

$$\text{Accruals} = (\text{change in total current assets} - \text{change in cash/equivalents})$$
$$- (\text{change in current liabilities} - \text{change in short-term debt})$$
$$- \text{change in income tax payable}) - \text{depreciation and amortization}$$

$$\text{Cash flow} = \text{Earnings} - \text{Accruals}$$

8.5.1 Income smoothing

I. Measure the variability of reported operating earnings to the variability of cash flows from operations, take the ratio (measure the variables relative to total assets). A low value is indicative of discretion being used to smooth reported earnings.
II. Contemporaneous correlation between accruals and operating cash flows (measured across firms). Large negative correlation implies the use of discretionary accruals to buffer cash flow shocks (use Spearman's rank correlation).

8.5.2 Discretion in reported earnings/size of acruals

I. Absolute accruals/absolute cash flows.
II. Small loss avoidance. Measure the incidence of small profits (relative to total assets) against the incidence of small losses (relative to total assets). A higher ratio indicates greater loss avoidance activity and hence greater earnings management.

8.6 TECHNICAL MEASURES

ARMS Index: (No. of advances/volume of advances)/(No. of declines/volume of declines)

HI/LO: No. of stocks at new highs/No. of stocks at new lows

A divergence often occurs as fewer and fewer stocks reach new heights, suggesting a petering out of sentiment, and hence a weak and vulnerable uptrend.

8.7   OTHERS

Cash flow into mutual funds

Level of cash in mutual fund

Herding: Given the discussion in Chapter 6 on self-imitation in markets, a measure of investor herding may be of use. We suggest using a measure proposed by Demirer and Lien (2001):

$$SD_i = \sqrt{\frac{\sum_{j=1}^{n} \left[\frac{(r_{j,t} - \bar{r}_t)}{r_t} \right]^2}{n-1}}$$

where n is the number of firms in the aggregate market portfolio, $r_{j,t}$ is the observed stock return for firm j on day t, $\bar{r}_t$ is the cross-sectional average of the n returns in the portfolio for day t.

Index compiled by Annette Musker